822-914 WIL

DICK BARTON

To Tim Winter
with all my love and respect

Phil Willmott

DICK BARTON – SPECIAL AGENT

DICK BARTON AND THE CURSE
OF THE PHARAOH'S TOMB

OBERON BOOKS
LONDON

First published in 1999 by Oberon Books Ltd.
(incorporating Absolute Classics)
521 Caledonian Road, London N7 9RH
Tel: 020 7607 3637 / Fax: 020 7607 3629
e-mail: oberon.books@btinternet.com

A catalogue record for this book is available from the British Library.

ISBN: 1 84002 149 7

Cover image and design: Paton Walker

Back cover photograph: James Gill

Printed in Great Britain by Antony Rowe Ltd, Reading.

Contents

DICK BARTON – SPECIAL AGENT

Characters

DICK BARTON

SNOWY WHITE

JOCK ANDERSON

MARTA HEARTBURN

DAPHNE FRITTERS

BARON SCARHEART

BBC ANNOUNCER

COLONEL GARDENER

VIPER'S NEST MC

SIR STANLEY FRITTERS

LADY LAXINGTON

RODGER

WILCO

CONVICTS

GANGSTERS

CABARET GIRLS

HACKS

Dick Barton – Special Agent was commissioned by the Warehouse Theatre Company and first performed at the Warehouse Theatre, Croydon, on 11 December 1998, with the following cast:

DICK BARTON/SNOWY*, Andrew C. Wadsworth

JOCK, Nicholas Tigg

MARTA/DAPHNE, Kate Graham

BARON SCARHEART, Mark Mckerracher

BBC ANNOUNCER/COLONEL, Sean Sloan

MC/SIR STANLEY/LADY LAXINGTON,
    Duncan Wisbey

Other characters played by members of the cast

*It is essential that Snowy is played by the same actor
    who plays Dick Barton

Director, Ted Craig

Designer, Michael Pavelka

Musical Director, Stefan Bednarczyk

Lighting, Leonard Tucker

The production was revived in June 1999 in a revised version with the following changes of cast:

BARON SCARHEART, Mark Roper

MARTA/DAPHNE, Sophie-Louise Dann

JOCK, Cymon Allen

BBC ANNOUNCER/COLONEL, Phillip Gates

Lighting, Douglas Kuhrt and Helen Morley

Costumes, Andri Korniotis

It is strongly suggested that the principle roles are doubled as in the original production

MUSICAL NUMBERS

Unless otherwise stated, all lyrics by Phil Willmott

ACT ONE

MARTA'S S.O.S
Music: by Stephan Bednarczyk
Marta

THE MOTTO OF THE BARTONS
Music: 'Rule Britannia' by Arne
Dick Barton & Reporters

THE CHOSEN ONES
Music: 'Nessun Dorma' by Puccini
Scarheart & Gang

THE PLAN
Music: 'The Hall of the Mountain King'
by Grieg
Scarheart

MARTA'S HEARTBURN
Music: 'Tit Willow' by Sullivan
Marta

EVERYTHING STOPS FOR TEA
Music and lyrics by Sigler/Hoffman/Goodhart
Additional lyrics by Willmott
Scarheart, Snowy, Daphne, Lady Laxington

ACT TWO

MARTA'S NIGHTCLUB
    Music: by Stephan Bednarczyk
    Marta & Girls

THE PHENOMENON
    Music: from 'The Pirates of Penzance' by Sullivan
    BBC Announcer & Dick Barton

A NIGHTINGALE SANG IN BERKERLEY SQUARE
    Music and lyrics by Manning/Sherwin
    Additional lyrics by Willmott
    Jock & Daphne

HAPPY FEET
    Music and lyrics by Ager/Yellen
    Dick Barton, Daphne, Jock & Sir Stanley

ACT ONE

Scene 1

A BBC ANNOUNCER appears in evening dress.

BBC ANNOUNCER: This is the BBC broadcasting from London. It's 6.45 and time for the next exciting instalment of Dick Barton, Special Agent.
(The Devil's Gallop – *the Dick Barton signature tune – starts.*)
Yesterday we left our hero at the mercy of arch villain Baron Scarheart. What infernal end has the rotter in mind for our hero? Can he escape to once again protect the free world from the forces of darkness?
(*We see an abandoned warehouse. DICK BARTON is suspended upside down at the end of a chain above an open trap door. His enemy, BARON SCARHEART, gloats. SCARHEART is eating an apple. There is a persistent dripping sound.*)

SCARHEART: So Dick Barton, at last the moment I have been waiting for. Soon your meddling will be over and London will be mine. Say your prayers Mr Secret Agent and prepare to die.

DICK BARTON: You won't get away with this Scarheart.

SCARHEART: And who's going to stop me? Your dim-witted sidekicks Jock and Snowy? It's because of their stupidity that you're in my power. With you out of the way they're just a pair of blithering idiots. Nothing can save you now, so why don't you relax and savour with me the prospect of your violent painful death?

DICK BARTON: What are you going to do?

SCARHEART: Can you hear a dripping sound?

DICK BARTON: What is it?

SCARHEART: Your last moments ebbing away. A tiny hole in the water tank above us releases a relentlessly slow trickle of water into an aluminium bucket. When it becomes exactly two-thirds full the weight of the water will tip it over a small tabby cat who will suddenly notice a three-legged hamster called Neville confined within a spinning drum and endeavour to reach it. The startled rodent will begin to run causing the drum to rotate. In exactly 2.3 minutes Neville will reach optimum speed causing the outside of the drum to spark against a strategically positioned flint, igniting the flame that will light a fuse connected to a small explosive device which upon detonation will release the winch from which you are suspended and you will be lowered inexorably into the mechanism beneath us.

DICK BARTON: What's the cat's name?

SCARHEART: Dwight.

DICK BARTON: Thank you, I like to get the whole picture.

SCARHEART: Quite so. The mechanism is where the real fun begins.

DICK BARTON: What infernal device have you conjured from the depths of hell?

SCARHEART: Allow me to demonstrate. (*He pulls a lever. A terrific whirring and clanking noise from beneath the trap door.*) Three tons of razor-sharp rotating steel blades. Enough to produce diced Dick for a Barton bolognaise within five delicious, deadly seconds. (*He throws his apple into the trap door. It spits the bits back out at him.*)

DICK BARTON: What kind of a monster are you? Is there no mercy in your heart?

SCARHEART: I have no heart. I was brought up by wolves on the Bavarian mountainside. Then when they couldn't cope with me any longer they sent me to Eton. Imagine the embarrassment. Other children received boxes of tuck, my family sent me roadkill – and that was only when they remembered. Never anything at Christmas. And now you will pay the price for their cruelty. I only wish I could stay to enjoy your suffering but tonight is the most important night in the criminal calendar. The annual (*Pronouncing each individual letter.*) E.F.I.L. dinner and dance.

DICK BARTON: (*Pronouncing the initials as a word.*) EFIL? What dastardly initials are those?

SCARHEART: The society of Evil Foreigners In London. How thrilled they will be to learn of your demise and to bathe in the twilight of a new darkness for our city. Farewell Barton. I hope you won't be hanging around for too long. (*His devilish laugh turns to the howl of a wolf. He sweeps out as DICK BARTON struggles.*)

Scene 2

The Viper's Nest nightclub in Soho.

The nightclub MC addresses the audience from the stage.

MC: Good evening and welcome to The Viper's Nest nightclub, exclusive haunt of the lowdown and downright despicable. Leave your morals outside. The audience is ugly, the girls are ugly, even the orchestra is ugly. The Viper's Nest is proud to be the home of EFIL and I'm thrilled to see so many frightening faces from international crime here tonight. Without further ado let's give a Viper's Nest welcome to the woman who's devastated the British Secret Service more or less single-handed – and you should see what she does with the other hand! She's flying back to Berlin directly after her appearance tonight! Our spy in their flies! Miss Marta Heartburn!
(*MARTA appears for her cabaret number. A beautiful, deadly vamp.*)

Marta's S.O.S.

MARTA: (*Sings.*)

DAMSELS ARE DISTRESSING
THIS ONE'S S.O.S.ING
WON'T SOMEBODY HEAR MY PLEA?
HELP WITH MY RESEARCHES
AND MY DESPERATE SEARCHES
FOR A MAN TO HANDLE ME

RICH MAN, POOR MAN
ANY MOTHER'S SON

I'VE MADE MINCEMEAT OUT OF EVERY ONE
WHEN I GET DEMANDING
THEY RUN FOR THE LANDING
WHERE'S THE MAN CAN HANDLE ME?

A DUKE SPENT MANY HOURS
BRINGING FLOWERS
I DEFLOWERED HIM
THEN DEVOURED HIM

A POSTAL CLERK ADDRESSED ME
THEN UNDRESSED ME
NOW HE SHARES HIS BED
WITH A MAN INSTEAD

MILLIONAIRES ALL SPEND THEIR LOT THEN LEAVE ME BLUE
SOLDIERS SHOOT BEFORE I'M THROUGH

SO I BEG YOU SISTER
CAN YOU SPARE YOUR MISTER?
GEN'RAL, SEND YOUR CAVALRY
THOUGH IT'S MY UNDOING
I'LL KEEP INTERVIEWING
FOR A MAN TO HANDLE ME

RICH MAN, POOR MAN
ANY MOTHER'S SON
I'VE MADE MINCEMEAT OUT OF EVERY ONE
HOW I LONG TO SETTLE
WITH A MAN OF METTLE
WHERE'S THE MAN CAN HANDLE ME?

(*At the end of the number, SCARHEART brings her a bouquet of flowers and she exits blowing kisses to the crowd. SCARHEART holds up his hand for silence.*)

SCARHEART: My fellow conspirators in EFIL, today our dream of world domination took one step further towards reality. I bring you glad tidings. Dick Barton, Special Agent, wireless celebrity and sworn enemy of infamy is dead. His end was a master-class in sadism. I think you might appreciate a little demonstration.

(*A model of DICK BARTON's death machine is wheeled out.*)

As I speak to you now, the following delicious horror unfolds in an East End warehouse.

(*A model DICK BARTON is lowered on a chain into a model meat grinder. SCARHEART turns the handle and mincemeat spews out of the other end. All this accompanied by music like a cheesy magic act.*)

My friends, nothing can stop us now. London is ours for the taking.

(*A sinister and grizzled figure has appeared at the back of the nightclub audience.*)

STRANGER: Not so fast Scarheart.

SCARHEART: What's this? Dissent from the floor? Welcome my friend. May I assume from your sinister countenance that you are a fellow disciple of EFIL?

STRANGER: Such a flawed plan could never destroy the great Dick Barton. The secret agent and tea-time radio star would simply climb up the chain, detach himself and then drop the chain down into the mechanism, blunting and snapping the blades. A simple technique he first used in *The Mystery of the Maharja's Bunion* if my memory serves me correctly.

SCARHEART: Just a moment, you know rather too much about Barton for my liking. There's something wrong here. (*He sneezes.*) Achooo! (*Looks pained.*)

STRANGER: (*Terribly nice.*) Bless you! My goodness I do hope you haven't caught a nasty chill.

SCARHEART: (*Triumphantly strong again.*) I thought so! There's not an ounce of EFIL in your body. (*He calls backstage.*) Ghouls, grab this imposter.

STRANGER: An imposter indeed. (*Ripping off his disguise.*) It is I, Dick Barton, and your cronies have already been rounded up by the police. Ably led by my colourful cockney assistant, Snowy White. All that remains is for you to give yourself up Baron...

(*SCARHEART pulls out a gun.*)

SCARHEART: Never!

(*But JOCK ANDERSON appears on stage behind SCARHEART and puts a gun to the villain's head.*)

JOCK: Don't worry boss, I've got him covered.

DICK BARTON: Ah, my second loyal assistant, Jock Anderson. They breed 'em tough in bonny Scotland but they'll sleep safer in Abergaveny tonight knowing you're behind bars, Baron.

JOCK: Abergaveny's in Wales, chief.

DICK BARTON: Same sort of thing, though.

JOCK: Come along Baron.

SCARHEART: I'll be back, you and your colourful working class sidekicks haven't seen the last of me.

(*JOCK leads SCARHEART out. HACKS rush in.*)

HACK: Harry Splat, *The Times.* Once again you've cheated death and thwarted evil Mr Barton. How do you do it?

HACK: Yes what's your secret Barton?

HACK: Will we be hearing about this case on your radio show?

HACK: Any message to inspire the people of Britain in these dark times?

DICK BARTON: My goodness me, what I do isn't so extraordinary. I'm only doing what Bartons have always done down the centuries. (*Sings.*)

The Motto of the Bartons

WHEN I WAS A LITTLE BOY MY FATHER SAID
OUR FAMILY'S ALWAYS STOOD AND FACED
THE FOES THAT WE MOST DREAD
SO TO THIS DAY I NEVER RUN AWAY
AND MEET THINGS HEAD TO HEAD

THE MOTTO OF THE BARTONS
IS 'GIVE EACH JOB YOUR BEST,
KEEP A STIFF UPPER LIP
AND ALWAYS WEAR A VEST.
PACK A TOOTHBRUSH,
AND CHANGE YOUR UNDERWEAR,
EAT AN APPLE EVERY DAY,
AND COMB YOUR HAIR.'

EVERYONE: (*Sings.*)

> HAIL DICK BARTON, A SPIFFING SORT OF CHUM
> BRITAIN NEVER, NEVER, NEVER SHALL SUCCUMB

DICK BARTON: (*Sings.*)

> HAPPY AND GLORIOUS IS MY ANCESTRY
> MY FAMILY SINCE THE DAWN OF TIME
> HAS LED THE VICTORY.
> FROM AGINCOURT TO WATERLOO
> WE'VE SUNG OUR EULOGY
>
> WE ARE THE BARTONS
> WE GIVE EACH JOB OUR BEST,
> WE KEEP A STIFF UPPER LIP
> AND ALWAYS WEAR A VEST.
> WERE'S MY TOOTHBRUSH,
> I'VE CHANGED MY UNDERWEAR,
> EATEN AN APPLE EVERY DAY,
> AND COMBED MY HAIR.

EVERYONE: (*Sings.*)

> HAIL DICK BARTON, HE'S AWFULLY, AWFULLY BRAVE
> BRITON'S NEVER, NEVER, NEVER...
> (*Big "Last Night of the Proms" finish.*)
> ...SHALL BE SLAVES.

(*HACKS leave. A telephone rings. DICK BARTON descends into the audience and picks up a flower from a table arrangement.*)

DICK BARTON: (*To the people at the table.*) Will you excuse me? (*Into the flower/phone.*) Barton here.
(*We can see COLONEL GARDENER on the other end of the telephone.*)

COLONEL: Colonel Gardener here, British Intelligence.

DICK BARTON: What can I do for you, Colonel?

COLONEL: I have a mission for you. A matter of tip-top priority. We're losing too many of our agents to the ruthless spy Marta Heartburn. We want you to travel to Berlin incognito and put an end to her hanky-panky.

DICK BARTON: I'm at The Viper's Nest. Marta was here half an hour ago.

COLONEL: She's one of EFIL's most valuable weapons. They'll be whisking her back to Berlin even as we speak. You must go after her but for heaven's sake, don't let anyone know you're on the case.

DICK BARTON: I get the picture. Anything else?

COLONEL: Secret agents Rodger and Wilco send their regards.

DICK BARTON: Rodger and Wilco?

COLONEL: Over and out.

(*JOCK returns.*)

JOCK: Snowy's on his way sir. They're having a bit of trouble getting Scarheart to the police station. A gang of wolves escaped from London zoo and tried to mount a rescue bid.

DICK BARTON: Extraordinary. But never mind about that. Colonel Gardener is sending me to Berlin on a top secret mission. I want you and Snowy to cover for me. No one must know I've left the country, no one must even know I've left the house. I want you to tell anyone who asks that I'm in bed with a nasty cold. Do you understand?

JOCK: A nasty cold. I think I've got that DB.

BARTON: Excellent. Then the security of the nation is safe in your hands.

BBC ANNOUNCER: And so our hero sets out on the most perilous mission of his career, deep into the heart of enemy territory. Meanwhile, British justice is swift and terrible to those who break its laws and Baron Scarheart and his gang soon find themselves sentenced to hard labour on Dartmoor.

Scene 3

A chain gang on Dartmoor.

SCARHEART: That it should come to this. Europe's most fiendish criminal minds breaking up rocks. Barton won't get away with it. He doesn't realise who he's dealing with, eh, lads? We're the worst.

CONVICT: We used to be. Now look at us.

CONVICT: Don't be downhearted. Scum always rises to the surface eventually.

CONVICT: I'm not so sure any more.

CONVICT: When I think of the old days I could cry.

CONVICT: They were wonderful times. We were disgusting. And now thanks to that smug bleeder Dick Barton we're all washed up.

CONVICT: We might get on the wireless though.

EVERYONE ELSE: Oh shut up!

CONVICT: (*To SCARHEART.*) When are we going to escape Baron? What are we going to do?

SCARHEART: Why is it always me who has to think up the escape plan?

CONVICT: Because you're the wickedest man in the universe.

CONVICT: And you're mean and nasty to us if we don't do what you say.

SCARHEART: And what does it all add up to, eh? What's my reward for years of terrorising the less criminally gifted? (*Sings.*)

Stress and Trauma

STRESS AND TRAUMA

STRESS AND TRAUMA

CONVICT: (*Spoken.*) Aint you got a plan then?

SCARHEART: (*Spoken.*) I just need some inspiration.

A MOTHER WOLF DID REAR ME

KNOWING MEN WOULD FEAR ME

THOUGH OLD AND TOOTHLESS

SHE STILL WAS CRUEL AND RUTHLESS

WHAT DID SHE SING US?

(*A howl from offstage.*)

SCARHEART: (*Spoken.*) Mother? Is that you? Your words. They're coming back to me.

WE ARE THE EVIL CHOSEN ONES

ALTHOUGH IT SEEMS THE VIRTUOUS HAVE WON

THERE'S ALWAYS SUN

BEFORE THE THUNDER
THE FINAL BATTLE'S YET TO COME

WE CAN'T GO WRONG LADS
JUST SING HER SONG LADS
STAND TALL AND STRONG LADS

ALL: (*Sing softly. Exquisite harmony.*)

WE ARE THE SCUMBAGS OF THE EARTH
OUR PARENTS WISH THEY'D STRANGLED US AT BIRTH

SCARHEART: (*Sings.*)

WE'LL FIGHT AGAIN THEN, WE CAN BITE AGAIN MEN
LET OUR WOLF MUSIC FILL THE WORLD WITH FEAR
HOWL IT LOUD AND HOWL IT CLEAR

ALL: (*Sing.*)

WE ARE THE EVIL CHOSEN ONES
ALTHOUGH IT SEEMS THE VIRTUOUS HAVE WON
THERE'S ALWAYS SUN
BEFORE THE THUNDER
THE FINAL BATTLE'S YET TO COME

(*They finish on a wolf howl.*)

GUARD: (*Off.*) All right, that's enough noise from you lot. Here's your lunch and as it's the governor's birthday he's letting you have a food parcel somebody left for you at the gates. Looks like foreign muck to me.

(*A food hamper is thrown on.*)

CONVICT: 'Ere Baron there's a note inside addressed to you. From M.H.

SCARHEART: Marta! I knew she wouldn't let me down.

CONVICT: (*Reads.*) 'A big Bavarian sausage for my big Bavarian sausage.'

SCARHEART: Give that to me. I want you all to distract the guard for a moment.

CONVICT: (*To the GUARD.*) Oi mate, who's got the best legs out of the Andrews Sisters?

GUARD: (*Off.*) That's a tricky one and no mistake.

CONVICT: I've got some pictures here.

(*The CONVICTS all exit to look at the pictures with the GUARD.*)

SCARHEART: (*Taking out a letter.*) Dear Baron, there is no time to waste. Escape from that nasty prison at once. I have stumbled upon a master plan that will make us the richest crooks in history and conquer the world. I will get details to you at The Viper's Nest. Meanwhile, use this sausage to aid your release. (*To himself.*) To aid our release?

MARTA: (*Unseen.*) It's a bomb you idiot!

(*SCARHEART turns the end of the sausage. We hear a loud ticking.*)

GUARD: (*Entering.*) Me and the lads have had a bit of a conflab about the Andrews Sisters question and we reckon it would have to be Laverne.

SCARHEART: My friend, in the interest of peace and harmony between our two nations might I invite you to share a little of this Bavarian delicacy?

GUARD: Well, it's a long time since there's been any delicacies round here. (*Takes the sausage.*) What is it?

SCARHEART: It is finest Bavarian sausage.

GUARD: Thank you very much. I've got a nice bit of mustard out the back. T'go lovely with that.

SCARHEART: Oh you won't be needing any mustard, my friend.

GUARD: A bit spicy on the old taste buds is it?

SCARHEART: Just a little. (*He exits.*)

GUARD: Ooh lovely (*Bites it.*)

(*Blackout. The sound of the dynamite exploding.*)

BBC ANNOUNCER: And so the most desperate criminals in Europe engineer their escape. Meanwhile, in Berlin the evil temptress Marta Heartburn has discovered that the new fly in her web is none other than Dick Barton, special agent.

Scene 4

MARTA's boudoir in Berlin.

MARTA: Who?

DICK BARTON: Barton, Dick Barton. Special agent. I've got my own radio programme. It's on at tea-time. You know…(*Sings a snatch of his theme.*)

MARTA: How wonderful. I must have you autograph something personal.

(*She raises her dress to extract a pencil from her garter.*)

DICK BARTON: If you make another move I'll shoot.

MARTA: I often have that effect on men.

DICK BARTON: Don't think I'm going to fall for any of your *femme fatale* nonsense. I won't be distracted from ensuring the safety of my country, its people and our beloved Royal Family.

MARTA: Most admirable Mr Barton but you are a long way from home, why don't you relax a little?

DICK BARTON: I need only think of the little princess Elizabeth and my resolve stiffens.

MARTA: You Englishmen are so strange. So proper, so reserved. Tell me Mr Barton. Have you ever been with a woman before?

DICK BARTON: Been where?

MARTA: Anywhere.

DICK BARTON: Actually, my nanny used to take me to Kensington Gardens. What's that got to do with anything?

MARTA: Oh Mr Barton, how much I could teach you. Or can I call you Herr Dick?

DICK BARTON: Special Agent Barton will be quite sufficient, thank you. And I learnt everything I need to know at British public school.

MARTA: Of course you did. Please forgive me. It's that nasty gun; it makes me so nervous.

DICK BARTON: Probably because you're a girl.

MARTA: Yes, yes I am. How perceptive of you Mr Barton. Beneath this haunted, racked exterior beats the heart of a frightened little girl. See, I'm trembling. You're so big and strong Mr Barton you don't need a gun to overpower me. I think…I think I'm going to faint.

DICK BARTON: There, there. No need for that. I'll put this away as long as you promise not to try any funny business.

MARTA: How could my frail little body ever hope to overpower an athlete like you?

DICK BARTON: You're probably right. Very well, but I'm going to have to cuff you. (*He searches in his pockets.*) There's a pair of handcuffs in here somewhere.

MARTA: Would you like to borrow mine?

DICK BARTON: That won't be necessary, thank you.

MARTA: So masterful. But before you discipline me, please might I smoke a last cigarette?

DICK BARTON: I don't see what harm it can do. Allow me. (*He offers her a cigarette.*)

MARTA: Oh no. I prefer to smoke my own. They have medicinal properties. (*She produces a big fat joint.*)

DICK BARTON: Goodness me. What a funny-looking smoke.

MARTA: Oh, my hands are trembling so. Would you light if for me?

DICK BARTON: Of course. (*He lights the cigarette and in doing so has to take a drag.*) Good heavens, what an unusual taste.

MARTA: That will be the herbs. I get these hand-rolled for me in the Chinese quarter. I think it's gone out. Would you be so kind?

DICK BARTON: Of course. (*He takes another drag.*) Medicinal you say?

MARTA: Oh yes, can't you feel your tensions drifting away?

DICK BARTON: Actually, I have been feeling a bit tense recently. Do you mind if I...

MARTA: Please help yourself.
(*He takes another drag.*)

DICK BARTON: Crikey! You know I think these little devils could be a valuable weapon in our war against the common cold.
(*MARTA begins to massage DICK BARTON.*)

MARTA: There, can you feel your muscles relax?

DICK BARTON: Absolutely. This is spiffing. Goodness me, you have got a delicate touch.

MARTA: Take another puff Mr Barton. Just let your muscles relax, relax, relax.

DICK BARTON: Oh dear!

MARTA: What is it?

DICK BARTON: I think the bally stuff has stopped working. I'm experiencing a certain isolated rigidity.
(*During the following she keeps placing the joint in his mouth. He smokes more and more.*)

MARTA: Oh that naughty side effect. That can sometimes happen. Why don't we take your handcuffs into my little playroom and I'll see what I can do to make everything alright.

DICK BARTON: Did you say playroom? I'm a British secret agent abroad on a mission. I've got no time for games.

MARTA: Oh I'm sure I can tempt you to a little Travel Scrabble. (*She leads him off, dangling the handcuffs.*)

BBC ANNOUNCER: Three weeks later Dick Barton has still not emerged from the playroom. Meanwhile, Scarheart's gang has gripped the East End of London in a terrible crime wave. Unchecked by Barton, the criminals thrive and Baron Scarheart gathers them all together at The Viper's Nest to outline Marta's diabolical new plan.

Scene 5

The Viper's Nest nightclub.

SCARHEART sings to his Viper's Nest audience.

The Plan

WELCOME TO MY LITTLE DEN
EFIL'S CRÈME DE LA CRÈME
MY CONGRATULATIONS
ON A CRIME WAVE THAT'S SUBLIME.
YOU HELLISH BREED,
YOU CHEATING FEW,
I'VE DEVISED SOMETHING NEW
A SCHEME THAT IS A SYMPHONY
OF INFAMY AND CRIME.

SO THEN, COMRADES
LISTEN CALM AND COLDLY
TO YOUR LEADER'S MASTER PLAN
AND BY CHRISTMAS
EFIL WILL BE TERRORISING
EV'RY ENGLISH MAN.

BRITISH PEOPLE CONSTANTLY
CRAVE FOR A CUP OF TEA
MORNING, NOON AND NIGHT TIME
THEY ARE BOILING UP A BREW.
WHITEHALL FEARS MORALE WOULD DIP
IF THEIR TEA STOCKS WERE HIT
SO EACH CITY'S TEA IS
HIDDEN SAFELY OUT OF VIEW.

MARTA HEARTBURN'S
DISCOVERED THE LOCATION OF THE LONDON
TEA SUPPLY
AND WE'RE GOING TO
TAMPER WITH THE TEA
AND WATCH OUR VICTIMS GETTING HIGH.

MARTA OFFERS CANNABIS
WHEN A MAN PLANS A KISS
SOON THEY'RE AT HER MERCY
AND SHE HAS HER WICKED WAY.
THIS IS SLUNK, HER STRONGEST DOPE
AND IT IS THIS WE HOPE
TO BE ADDING TO THE NATION'S
CUPPA EVERY DAY.

WE MUST KIDNAP THE
ONLY MAN WHO KNOWS
WHERE BRITAIN'S OTHER TEA IS STORED.
THEN WE'LL ADD SLUNK
GET THE COUNTRY STONED
AND STEAL OURSELVES A MASSIVE HOARD.

SO WE NEED A TRIAL RUN
AND THE PLAN HAS BEGUN
TOMORROW WE WILL TAMPER WITH

AOME HIGH SOCIE-TEAS
WE'LL BE CAUSING QUITE A STIR
DOWN IN BELGRAVIA
WHEN I SERVE REFRESHMENTS
THAT WILL BRING THEM TO THEIR KNEES.

(*He howls like a wolf.*)

BBC ANNOUNCER: Can this dreadful infamy be allowed to strike at the cream of London society? Are the nation's top people to remain unprotected? At Dick Barton's HQ an angry mob of plucky working-class folk collect outside, demanding the intervention of their hero. The warmth of their simple uneducated belief in the special agent no doubt warming the cockles of their humble cockney hearts.

Scene 6

Barton HQ.

JOCK is leaning out of the window listening to the crowd. SNOWY WHITE is standing by.

SNOWY: What are they saying about Mr Barton now, Jock?

JOCK: Well, Snowy they say the governor's a poncy, good-for-nothing banker.

SNOWY: Banker?

JOCK: I think that was the word. I wish they'd go home. It's getting late and they're frightening his homely housekeeper Mrs Horrock.

SNOWY: Aint they got no respect for his nibs? He's a bleedin' 'ero. He's proved 'isself dozens of times. They wanna remember that.

JOCK: Snowy, how long have we been Dick Barton's assistants now?

SNOWY: Love a duck, I reckon it's nigh on five year and no mistake.

JOCK: I don't remember him ever disappearing like this. I'm afeared something awful bad's happened to him.

SNOWY: He'll be in touch soon.

JOCK: Do you think so?

SNOWY: We've got to keep believing that any minute now we'll get a tinkle on the old dog and bone. We can't give up 'ope. What would we tell that lot outside?

JOCK: What are we going to tell them anyway?

SNOWY: We could tell them his temperature's gone down a bit?

JOCK: We did that last Wednesday, I'm getting desperate. How long can we keep up this story that he's in bed with flu?

SNOWY: You told them it was that 'orrible Russian sort.

JOCK: Russian, Mongolian, Bratislavian, I'm running out of flu types.

SNOWY: Presbyterian?

JOCK: We're not supposed to have to think of things. That's for the nobs like the Colonel and DB. I answered an advert for strong armed working-class type with an amusing regional accent. It didn't say anything about thinking up plans.

SNOWY: Well, we've got to tell 'em something before they start breaking the windows.

JOCK: They're your clan. Can't you think of something that'll impress them?

SNOWY: I'll try. If that don't work I'll just thump a few of 'em. (*He goes.*)

JOCK: (*Alone.*) Come on DB. Get in touch. Where can you be? We need you, your country needs you.
(*There is a knock at the door.*)
Come in Mrs Horrock. Is there any news?
(*DAPHNE FRITTERS enters. Pale, stiff upper-lipped English rose. She is willowy and beautiful, virginal and innocent, the complete opposite of MARTA. She has a 'Brief Encounter' accent.*)

DAPHNE: Your housekeeper said I might disturb you.

JOCK: Oh absolutely Miss, won't you sit down?

DAPHNE: Thank you. My name is Daphne Fritters. I must say Mr Barton you don't look anything like your picture in the Radio Times.

JOCK: Och no lassie. I'm not Dick Barton. Mr Barton is in the bedroom.

DAPHNE: But it's only seven o'clock.

JOCK: He's been in bed all day with the Presbyterian type.

DAPHNE: My goodness. Would it be possible to intrude?

JOCK: I'm afraid not. He's getting it good and proper. That bedroom door's been locked for three weeks.

DAPHNE: But this is an emergency.

JOCK: I'm afraid I can't disturb him. Strict instructions.

DAPHNE: Then all is lost. (*She cries daintily into a little lace handkerchief.*)

JOCK: Don't cry Miss. There's nothing to be done. This Presbyterian type will have anyone on their back.

DAPHNE: Thank you for the warning. Well, I can tell from your endearing regional accent that you must be Jock. Please can you help me? This is a national emergency and you seem so kind and honourable and…rugged.

JOCK: Well, why don't I write it down and then I can pass it on to Mr Barton when he's up and about.

DAPHNE: Oh could you? I've nowhere else to turn.
(*JOCK attempts to write down what she says.*)
It's about my father Sir Stan Fritters. He's Minister for Rationing. Or he was…or still is…or…I don't know any more. You see he's missing. Well not missing without trace…I mean he left a note…but he…Oh, it's all too terrible. If only mother were still alive but she was killed in an horrific croquet accident and ever since then Daddy and I have been completely alone and now he's gone and I don't know what to do or where to turn or how to make toast or anything and – (*Suddenly aware that JOCK is not writing.*) Are you getting all this down?

JOCK: Does rationing have one "n" or two?

DAPHNE: Would you like me to go slower?

JOCK: Would you mind? It's just I'm the gruff, salt of the earth, physical type.

DAPHNE: How refreshing. Well I'll try to be clearer and look deep into your piercing blue eyes as I speak. My father is responsible for war-time provisions and I'm proud to say

(*She is getting a little distracted from staring into JOCK's eyes.*)
that the country can feel very safe in his strong masculine
arms...Anyway, three weeks ago I returned home from a
lacrosse tournament to find he'd left this note. (*She hands
JOCK the note. Then thinks better of it.*) Perhaps I'll read it
to you. 'Dear Daphers, Daddy has to go into hiding.
Am in great danger. I will contact you when the coast is
clear. Do not let any strangers into the house. Especially
not for tea.' What can it mean?

JOCK: Och, a hot refreshing beverage with perhaps a few
sandwiches and a slice of shortbread.

DAPHNE: Not the tea, the 'grave danger' bit. I haven't
heard from Daddy in nearly a month. I'm beside myself
with worry. I just sit at home all day and stare at the
phone, waiting for his call. (*Fast and breathless.*) In fact I
should be getting back there now. What if he's rung
while I've been here with you? Oh my goodness! Please,
you will ask Mr Barton to investigate won't you? I'm
sure with your help, Mr Jock, my father will be safely
home in no time. I know I can rely on you. (*Beat.*) Tell
me do hoary handed men of toil really have hoary hands?

JOCK: I try to keep my nails nice.

(*SNOWY returns.*)

DAPHNE: Oh Mr Barton, you've emerged. (*Whole speech
fast and breathless.*) Please, please will you help me?
I'm such a huge fan of your radio serial and I'm in such
a frightful scrape. I have to rush home now to wait for a
telephone call from my eminent father who's vital to the
survival of our country and who has disappeared under
mysterious circumstances. Mr Jock will fill you in on the
details. Oh heavens, poor Daddy!

JOCK: Wait, where can we reach you?

DAPHNE: Two two two Berkeley Square.

(*She rushes out.*)

SNOWY: An invitation has arrived for the guv. A tea party
at Lady Laxington's.

JOCK: Just a minute Snowy, there's an odd stirring in my
iron breast, a fluttering, a...I think it might be...love.

SNOWY: Butterflies in the stomach? (*JOCK nods.*) Ringin' in the ears? (*JOCK nods.*) Strange discomfort in the lower abdomen?

JOCK: Yes, that's right. Is it love?

SNOWY: Nah, mate it's indigestion. I get it all the time. Fancy her thinking I was a secret agent.

JOCK: She's seen DB's picture in the Radio Times. Just a minute. I've never noticed it before but you do look a bit like him.

SNOWY: 'Ere you 'avin me on?

(*JOCK holds up the photograph of DICK BARTON to SNOWY's face. They look identical.*)

JOCK: It's a very slight resemblance.

SNOWY: Yeh, but I couldn't do all the clever, brave things he does.

JOCK: No but we could pass you off as him for a few days. You could appear in a few places, then at least people would feel Dick Barton was on the case.

SNOWY: No one's gonna believe I'm the guv.

JOCK: Why not? We can teach you a few phrases and you can just drop them into conversation. Just a minute. That tea party invitation for the boss. When's that for?

SNOWY: The day after tomorrow.

JOCK: That will be the test. Let's see if we can pass you off as DB at Lady Laxington's.

SNOWY: That old battleaxe. She'll see through me in no time.

JOCK: No she won't. Not if you work hard. For a start you can read this.

SNOWY: What is it?

JOCK: I heard his nibs discussing it the other day. It's called *Pride and Prejudice.* It's all about gentlemen and ladies and a laddie called Mr Darcy. It'll show you what to do. Bye.

SNOWY: Where are you going?

JOCK: Berkeley Square.

SNOWY: What for?

JOCK: I'm going to make sure Miss Fritters gets home safely.

SNOWY: (*Reads.*) 'It is a truth universally acknowledged that a single man in possession of a fortune must be in want of a wife.'

BBC ANNOUNCER: Meanwhile, in old Berlin, Marta Heartburn finds that her conquest of Dick Barton has not gone as smoothly as she'd hoped. Something unexpected has happened…

Scene 7

Marta's Heartburn

MARTA: (*Sings.*)

OH WHAT'S THIS OBSESSION THAT'S SUDDENLY HIT?
I CANNOT STOP THINKING OF BARTON.
ON A TREE BY MY WINDOW A LITTLE TOM TIT
I SWEAR WAS REPEATING 'DICK BARTON'
THIS CHIRPY INSISTENCE WAS FILLING MY HEAD
SO I GOT A REVOLVER AND SHOT THE BIRD DEAD
BUT THE WHOLE BLOODY GARDEN JUST SANG IT INSTEAD
A LOVELY DAWN CHORUS OF BARTON.

I RAN TO THE PRIEST BEGGING "FATHER, OH PLEASE,
DELIVER THIS SINNER FROM BARTON."
BUT LATER I FOUND MYSELF BACK ON MY KNEES
I CAN'T GET ENOUGH OF DICK BARTON.
I'VE WHIPPED HIM AND HIT HIM
AND STARVED HIM FOR DAYS
AND HUMILIATED HIM HUNDREDS OF WAYS
BUT HE STILL SAYS 'GOOD MORNING' AND I'M IN A DAZE
DICK BARTON, DICK BARTON –

SAY IT LOUD AND A BAND IS PLAYING
SAY IT SOFT AND IT FEELS LIKE YOU'RE PRAYING
DICK BARTON, I'LL NEVER STOP SAYING –
DICK BARTON, DICK BARTON, DICK BARTON!

BBC ANNOUNCER: Meanwhile, in Belgravia, Lady Laxington is making final preparations for her tea party.

Scene 8

LADY LAXINGTON's drawing room in Belgravia.

LADY LAXINGTON: Parkinson! Parkinson!
  (*SCARHEART enters dressed as a butler.*)
LADY LAXINGTON: Who are you? You're not Parkinson.
  Where's my butler?
SCARHEART: There was an unfortunate accident, my
  lady. Parkinson was attacked by wolves in the lower
  pantry. I shall be your butler for this afternoon.
LADY LAXINGTON: Well, I hope you're up to the job, this
  is a very important tea party. The special agent Dick
  Barton is joining us to regale the ladies with tales of his
  daredevil exploits.
SCARHEART: How absolutely perfect. And who will the
  other guests be your ladyship? So that I might attend to
  any special requirements they may have.
LADY LAXINGTON: My dear friend Lady Porchester.
SCARHEART: (*To himself, scribbling in a pocketbook.*) Assets
  of about two million, houses in Kensington, Surrey and
  the Highlands, owner of the Porchester diamond and two
  large Holbeins.
LADY LAXINGTON: Lady Hammersmith is coming.
SCARHEART: One and a half million, three Vemeers, one
  Turner, much admired emerald necklace.
LADY LAXINGTON: Then there's the Duchess of Swithen,
  Lady Cranmere, Lady Hexton, Baroness Dunston, Lady
  Penrith and the Duchess of York. Young Daphne Fritters
  became very interested when she heard that Mr Barton
  was to address us.
SCARHEART: Daughter of Sir Stanley Fritters. He's the
  man who knows the location of all the British tea stocks.
  Barton and Fritters at the one tea party, we have struck
  gold indeed.
LADY LAXINGTON: What are you mumbling about man?
SCARHEART: I must select a very special tea for such an
  illustrious gathering. I think I know just the blend.

LADY LAXINGTON: We drink Earl Grey in this house. I hope you are not from the modern vulgar school of butlering.
(*The doorbell rings.*)
Ah, that will be Mr Barton now. Please send him straight up.

SCARHEART: Very good, my lady.

LADY LAXINGTON: And ask the other guests to wait in the blue room.

SCARHEART: Yes, my lady.

LADY LAXINGTON: Hurry up man, we don't want to keep dear Mr Barton waiting.
(*SNOWY bursts into the room disguised as DICK BARTON, except he actually looks more like Mr Darcy.*)

SNOWY: Fear not ma'am, it is a truth universally acknowledged that it is I.

SCARHEART: (*Announcing the guest.*) Dick Barton, my lady.

SNOWY: I took the liberty of forcing my company unbidden upon you. Forgive my callowness, I beg of you dear Elizabeth. In vain have I struggled, it will not do. My feelings will not be repressed. You must allow me to tell you how ardently I admire and love you. Might I call you Elizabeth?

LADY LAXINGTON: Great heavens! No one has called me Elizabeth since my late husband.
(*The bell rings again.*)

SCARHEART: Excuse me, madame.

LADY LAXINGTON: (*Lusting for SNOWY.*) Shut the old biddies in the blue room until I've finished with Mr Barton.

SCARHEART: Very good madame. (*Gleefully.*) I shall serve them tea. (*He exits.*)

LADY LAXINGTON: Goodness, Mr Barton, your stridency has quite taken me by surprise.

SNOWY: You have a sweet room here, and a charming prospect over the gravel walk. You will not think of quitting it in a hurry.

LADY LAXINGTON: I'm so glad you like it. Of course I spend much of the year in the country.

SNOWY: Whatever I do is done in a hurry and therefore if I should resolve to quit the countryside, I should probably be off in five minutes. (*Offers her a cigarette.*) Fag?

LADY LAXINGTON: No thank you.

SNOWY: It is a truth universally acknowledged that a single man in possession of a snout must be in want of an ashtray.

(*DAPHNE bursts in.*)

DAPHNE: Forgive my intruding Lady Laxington but I need to speak to Mr Barton on a matter of some urgency.

LADY LAXINGTON: Ill-mannered girl, bursting in here without an introduction.

DAPHNE: Oh, but I have to speak to him. It is so rare to find Mr Barton without his Presbyterian friend. I feel so foolish intruding.

SNOWY: It does not necessarily follow that a deep intricate character is more or less estimable then such a one as yours.

DAPHNE: Mr Barton, you have to help me. My father could be in very great danger.

(*SCARHEART appears with tea things.*)

SCARHEART: Tea is served.

LADY LAXINGTON: I thought I told you to serve tea in the blue room?

SCARHEART: Tea is indeed being served there your ladyship. My colleagues are ensuring that your other guests are being catered for but I thought your ladyship, Mr Barton – oh! and Miss Fritters – might appreciate some refreshment. I think you'll find this particular tea most diverting.

LADY LAXINGTON: I've told you before, man, we drink Earl Grey in this household and nothing else.

SCARHEART: I'm sure your ladyship will be impressed – (*Sings.*)

Everything Stops For Tea

THIS IS REALLY VERY SPECIAL
I KNOW THAT YOU'LL ENJOY THE QUALITY

YOU'LL HAVE YOURSELF A BALL
WITH WHAT'S IN STORE –
(*LADY LAXINGTON takes a sip of tea and reacts pleasurably.*)
– EVERYTHING STOPS FOR TEA.

LADY LAXINGTON: (*Sings.*)

MY GOODNESS I'VE GONE GIDDY
I'M SPINNING EXTRAORDINARILY
I FEEL I COULD FLY
MR BARTON TRY –
(*SNOWY takes a sip of tea.*)
– EVERYTHING STOPS FOR TEA.

SNOWY: (*Sings. Cockney again.*)

"UNIVERSALLY ACKNOWLEDGED"
WHAT AM I ON ABOUT?
I'LL HAVE ANOTHER CUPPA
THE BREW IS REALLY PUCKA
LET'S NOT HANG ABOUT

LADY LAXINGTON/SNOWY: (*Sing.*)

WHAT IS THIS FUNNY FEELING?
I'M GRINNING LIKE A MONKEY UP A TREE.

LADY LAXINGTON: (*Sings.*)

IT'S SO AWFULLY QUEER
WON'T YOU JOIN US DEAR?

DAPHNE: (*Sings.*)

NO, I DON'T DRINK TEA

THE OTHERS: (*Sing.*)

WHAT!

SNOWY: (*Sings.*)

OH THE FACTORIES MAY BE ROARING
WITH A ZOOMALAKA, ZOOMALAKA –

LADY LAXINGTON: (*Sings.*)

WHEE!

SNOWY: (*Sings.*)

> BUT THERE ISN'T ANY ROAR
> WHEN THE CLOCK STRIKES FOUR

LADY LAXINGTON/SNOWY: (*Sing.*)

> EVERYTHING STOPS FOR TEA.

LADY LAXINGTON: (*Sings.*)

> IT'S A VERY GOOD ENGLISH CUSTOM
> THOUGH THE WEATHER BE COLD OR HOT
> IF YOU NEED A LITTLE PICK UP
> BE SURE A LITTLE TEA CUP
> WILL ALWAYS HIT THE SPOT.

SCARHEART: (*Sings.*)

> OH A LAWYER IN A COURTROOM
> IN THE MIDDLE OF AN ALIMONY PLEA
> HAS TO STOP AND LET IT FALL
> WHEN THE CLOCK STRIKES FOUR

LADY LAXINGTON/SNOWY/SCARHEART: (*Sing.*)

> EVERYTHING STOPS FOR TEA.

SNOWY: (*Sings.*)

> FROM CUPS OF FINEST CHINA
> IT'S THE TIPPLE OF THE ARISTOCRACY
> AND THE WORKING CLASS
> HAVE THEIR THERMOS FLASKS

LADY LAXINGTON/SNOWY/SCARHEART: (*Sing.*)

> EVERYTHING STOPS FOR TEA.

DAPHNE: (*Sings.*)

> FATHER IS IN TROUBLE
> WHY WILL NO ONE UNDERSTAND
> (*To SNOWY.*)
> HOW CAN YOU SIT SIPPING TEA
> WHEN DANGER STALKS THE LAND?
>
> GOODBYE LADY LAXINGTON
> FORGIVE ME IF I RUN

THERE'S A BONNY SCOTSMAN
I KNOW WILL GET THINGS DONE.
(*She exits.*)

SNOWY/LADY LAXINGTON: (*Sing.*)

WHEN A SCOTSMAN'S FEELING THIRSTY
WHISKY IS HIS PARTIALITY
BUT IT WON'T GIVE HIM A BUZZ
LIKE A TEA LEAF DOES
EVERYTHING STOPS FOR TEA.

EVERYONE: (*Sings.*)

DON'T TRUST A FANCY BEV'RAGE
NO MATTER IF IT HAS A PEDIGREE
WHO COULD ASK FOR MORE
WHEN THE CLOCK STRIKES FOUR
EVERYTHING STOPS FOR TEA!

(*THUGS enter and carry the comotose LADY LAXINGTON off leaving SCARHEART with SNOWY.*)

SCARHEART: So, Dick Barton, we meet again.

SNOWY: Tea for three and me for two, two for three and tea for toast. Toast, mmm...

SCARHEART: I see you enjoyed my special brand of tea?

SNOWY: Too bleedin' right.

SCARHEART: How exhilarating to hear that brilliant detective mind turning to mush.

SNOWY: Don't you mush me, Mush.

SCARHEART: The drug has made you putty in my hands.

SNOWY: I never liked it there.

SCARHEART: Where?

SNOWY: Putney.

SCARHEART: Putney?

SNOWY: In your hands.

SCARHEART: You. You are in my hands. Like putty.

SNOWY: How did we get there?

SCARHEART: Where?

SNOWY: Putney?

SCARHEART: Putty.

SNOWY: There's no such place as Putty. You're lost mate.

SCARHEART: I am not lost, I am in control.

SNOWY: I thought you was in Putney?

SCARHEART: NO!

SNOWY: Where am I?

SCARHEART: Safe with me.

SNOWY: Am I in control and all?

SCARHEART: No, I am in control.

SNOWY: You're in control?

SCARHEART: Oh yes.

SNOWY: And I'm in Putney?

SCARHEART: FORGET PUTNEY. NOBODY IS IN PUTNEY!

SNOWY: My Auntie Vi lives in Putney.

SCARHEART: Shut up. Shut up before I kill you.

SNOWY: You don't want to do that.

SCARHEART: No I don't. I want to interrogate you, tease out everything you know about the British Secret Service while your brain is putrid.

SNOWY: 'Ere! Don't you call me stupid.

SCARHEART: I said putrid.

SNOWY: (*Satisfied.*) Oh that's alright then. Ta very much.

SCARHEART: Why are you talking with a loutish demeanour?

SNOWY: I'll talk to anyone. (*Sniffs.*)

SCARHEART: Listen very carefully. Do the British have a secret weapon?

SNOWY: I don't know. The guv'nor don't tell me nothin'. (*Sneezes.*)

SCARHEART: 'The Guv'nor'? (*SNOWY sniffs again.*) Is that a code?

SNOWY: No, just a bit of a sniffle. You sound a bit bunged up though.

SCARHEART: DO YOU HAVE A CODE?

SNOWY: NO, I'M VERY WELL THANK YOU.

SCARHEART: This is extraordinary. The tea's turned you into a moron. It works better than I could possibly imagine. Boys! Get in here.
(*THUGS re-enter draped in tiaras and jewels.*)
Behold the worm that was Dick Barton!

SNOWY: Whatcha!

SCARHEART: Slunk has proved a powerful drug indeed.

A THUG: We've ransacked the whole house and all the old dears. We're getting away with a fortune.

SCARHEART: Excellent. Where are they now?

A THUG: Down in the kitchen. They've got very peckish all of a sudden.

SCARHEART: The side effects are very strange, Barton's turned Cockney.

A THUG: I tell you what, I'm staying off the Rosie Lee for a while.

SCARHEART: From now on it's champagne for us. My fellow freaks, did I not tell you we would rise triumphantly from the ashes?

A THUG: You've done us proud, boss.

SCARHEART: And tomorrow we make all EFIL proud. Once we have tortured the whereabouts of the rest of Britain's tea from Sir Stanley Fritters, we shall lace it with Slunk and Britain will be powerless to resist a foreign invasion. History will call it V. Tea day!

A THUG: That's brilliant, Baron.

ANOTHER THUG: Yeh, really evil.

SCARHEART: And all the information we need will be provided by Barton's raddled brain!

BBC ANNOUNCER: (*Theme under.*) And so EFIL's gleeful laughter rings out through the drawing rooms of Belgravia as the villains count their plunder. Is the whole of London's high society to be a grab-bag for infamy? Will Baron Scarheart's dastardly plot succeed? Where is Stan Fritters? Will Jock fall for Daphne? Will the real Dick Barton escape the clutches of Marta Heartburn and get home in time to save the free world? Tune in after the interval for the next exciting instalment of Dick Barton – Special Agent!

End of Act One.

ACT TWO

Scene 9

On stage in a Berlin nightclub.

MARTA is performing a nightclub act supported by CABARET GIRLS. All very Kit Kat Club.

Marta's Nightclub

MARTA: (*Sings. Slow and refined.*)

> THERE'S A PLACE I KNOW
> IT'S THE FINEST NIGHTSPOT
> IN ALL OF BERLIN.
> WHERE CROWNED HEADS OF EUROPE
> MUST TAKE THEIR CHANCE
> IN THE FIGHT TO GET IN.
> DINE ON TRUFFLES AND FINE CAVIAR,
> DANCE IN THE ARMS OF A GLAMOROUS STAR,
> WATCH THE BEAUTIFUL PEOPLE PASS,
> EVERYBODY REEKS OF CLASS.
> WHO KNOWS WHO MIGHT APPEAR
> NEATH THAT GRAND CHANDELIER.
> WELL THAT'S THERE
> THINGS ARE A LITTLE BIT DIFFERENT HERE.

GIRLS: (*Sing.*)

> WELCOME NAUGHTY BOY
> TO MARTA'S NIGHTCLUB
> IN DOWN TOWN BERLIN.

MARTA: (*Sings.*)

> THE GIRLS LONG TO MEET YOU
> SO STEP RIGHT UP, LET THE PARTY BEGIN.
> THERE ARE GIRLS WHO WILL BLO-OW YOU'RE MIND
> OR BLO-OW WHAT EVER IT IS THAT THEY FIND.

GIRLS: (*Sing.*)

> WE CAN PLAY OUT YOUR FANTASY

MARTA: (*Sings.*)

FOR A REASONABLE FEE.

GIRLS: (*Sing.*)

JUST SAY WHAT WE CAN DO
WE'LL ACCOMMODATE YOU

MARTA: (*Sings.*)

TAKE A CHANCE,

MARTA/GIRLS: (*Sing.*)

CASH IN ADVANCE AND WE DANCE ALL NIGHT THROUGH.

GIRLS: (*Sing.*)

WELCOME NAUGHTY BOY
TO MARTA'S NIGHTCLUB
IN DOWNTOWN BERLIN
WE'RE AN INSTITUTION,
A LONG ESTABLISHED
ORIGINAL SIN
SO THE DECOR IS TATTY AND CRUDE

MARTA: (*Sings.*)

THAT'S WHY WE KEEP ALL THE LIGHTING SUBDUED.

GIRLS: (*Sing.*)

THOUGH THE CARPET'S NONE TOO CLEAN

MARTA: (*Sings.*)

THE MIRRORS ON THE CEILINGS GLEAM.

GIRLS: (*Sing.*)

FOR THE DISCERNING FEW
ALL GOOD MEM'RIES ARE BLUE.

MARTA: (*Sings.*)

TAKE YOUR CHANCE
CASH IN ADVANCE AND WE DANCE ALL NIGHT THROUGH.

ALL: (*Sing.*)

CAN YOU?

(Backstage: one of the GIRLS is talking to MARTA. We can hear the crowd calling for more over the tannoy.)

CABARET GIRL: Marta, listen to that crowd. They are going mad for you. We must perform another encore. Shall I tell the band to strike up the comedy nun routine?

MARTA: No Helga, my heart is not in my performance tonight. I long to return to my beloved. This world seems so tawdry to me, how empty the painted smiles seem when my mind is full of Dick.

CABARET GIRL: Oh Marta, do you think somewhere there's a Dick for me?

MARTA: If only all the men in the world were like him. When we make love there is a lion in my bed, when we rest there is a lamb in my arms and when we kiss there is an electric eel in my –

CABARET GIRL: *(Starry-eyed.)* Does he know any funny stories?

MARTA: Oh, he can't talk, he's too stoned. A love god who does exactly what he's told and doesn't answer back.

CABARET GIRL: Every girl's dream. Shall I tell the girls you'll join us for a schnapps later?

MARTA: No Helga I have a date in the arms of the man I love. *(HELGA sighs. A radio crackles into life, fiendishly disguised as a bra amongst MARTA's costumes.)*

SCARHEART: *(Voice over the radio.)* Big Baron calling Mother Marta, Big Baron calling Mother Marta.

CABARET GIRL: What is that noise?

MARTA: Noise? What noise? It is probably the mice.

SCARHEART: Big Baron calling Mother Marta.

CABARET GIRL: There it is again. Do you hear it?

MARTA: That? That's my new ventriloquist act. I throw my voice so it sounds like it is coming from the other side of the room.

SCARHEART: Big Baron calling Mother Marta.

CABARET GIRL: It is so convincing. It sounds like it is coming from that brassiere. How do you do it?

MARTA: Oh just practice really, you start with a shoe perhaps, maybe a hat. In no time at all you're chatting to your bra. Now will you forgive me Helga. I'm rather busy.

CABARET GIRL: Oh Marta, may I just say how much
I admire you?

SCARHEART: Why don't you listen, you useless old slapper.

CABARET GIRL: Alright I'm going. I'm going. I thought
we were friends.

*(She rushes from the room in tears. MARTA puts the bra over
her head so that the cups become earphones.)*

MARTA: Mother Marta to Big Baron. I heard what you
called me you bull-headed oaf.

*(A dissolve to reveal SCARHEART on the other end of the
radio. Beside him is SNOWY, still disguised as DICK
BARTON, tied to a chair.)*

SCARHEART: Listen carefully my little sprig of deadly
nightshade. Your plan has worked a treat. In the last few
days we have cleaned out Knightsbridge, Belgravia and
Kensington. The British are putty in our hands.

MARTA: The signal's breaking up. What was that about
Putney?

SCARHEART: Soon EFIL will rule the world.

MARTA: Have you found the secret locations for the rest of
Britain's tea?

SCARHEART: Not yet. The minister has gone into hiding
but I have set our most ruthless thugs to track him down.

MARTA: Any trouble from the police?

SCARHEART: Without their leader they are headless
chickens. And that is my other piece of news, oh cataract
of my eye. I have captured Dick Barton.

MARTA: What do you mean?

SCARHEART: Dick Barton is in my power, laid low by the
power of Slunk.

MARTA: But Barton is here with me in Berlin.

SCARHEART: That cannot be. He is here at my side.

MARTA: Impossible. I have made him my personal love
slave, even now he attends to my every whim.

*(A figure encased in leather including a leather bondage mask
brings MARTA a cocktail and begins to kiss her feet and up
her leg.)*

SCARHEART: He is here I tell you. (*To SNOWY.*) I say, would you mind saying a few words to my friend? She's a huge fan of your wireless show.

SNOWY: (*Into the radio.*) It is a truth universally acknowledged that it is I.

MARTA: There's something very wrong here. (*Unzips the leather mask.*) Speak to me Dick.

SLAVE: (*Who is clearly not DICK BARTON.*) Gutten Tag!

MARTA: Who are you? Where is my Dick? (*She gives the SLAVE a good kick. He rolls over like a dog and pants.*) I have been tricked. Barton has escaped me. Keep him with you. I leave for London immediately. I must be reunited with him before dawn.

SCARHEART: (*To SNOWY.*) You're in for a long night.

SNOWY: (*Still stoned.*) Lovely jubbaly!

BBC ANOUNCER: All over Europe confusion reigns. Where is the real Dick Barton? Will he return in time to save the free world from the forces of EFIL? (*Sings.*)

The Phenomenon

THIS LOOKS BLEAK

NO HERO IS AT HAND

DARKNESS REIGNS

AND EFIL STALKS THE LAND

COAST TO COAST

THE NATION HOLDS ITS BREATH

HAS DICK BARTON MET A GRISLY DEATH?

(*DICK BARTON appears from nowhere.*)
DICK BARTON: (*Sings.*)

FEAR NOT

I'M ON MY WAY

ALL WILL BE REVEALED

NOTHING LEFT CONCEALED

I'LL WIN ANOTHER FIGHT

AND EVERYTHING WILL BE ALRIGHT!

MILLIONS GATHER

ROUND THE RADIO

IN SUSPENSE

THEY LISTEN TO MY SHOW

THEY'LL REJOICE

WHEN BARTON GETS HIS MAN

WINSTON CHURCHILL

IS A LOYAL FAN!

I'M A PHENOMENON

NO MAN SINGLE-HANDED

COULD DO WHAT THIS MAN DID

I'VE NEVER MET MY MATCH

WHATEVER PLAN

THE VILLAINS HATCH!

BBC ANNOUNCER: At Dick Barton's HQ Colonel Gardener of British Intelligence assesses the situation with typical allied pluck and initiative.

Scene 10

DICK BARTON's HQ.

COLONEL: (*Frantic.*) Oh my God! oh my God! What are we going to do! What do you mean you've lost two of them?

JOCK: Well, Snowy was disguised as Mr Barton to cover up for the guv while he was away, but he got kidnapped at Lady Laxington's tea party. Meanwhile there's been no news of the real Dick Barton.

COLONEL: This is terrible. If we don't find Barton soon there'll be an EFIL flag hanging from every British lamppost before Christmas. Well, desperate times call for desperate measures. I've placed an advertisement in *The Times* offering a thousand pound reward for Barton's safe return.

JOCK: Do you think that'll do the trick?

COLONEL: It has too, the man's a national treasure. Without his tea-time radio show morale's slumped to an all-time low. (*He produces a chart demonstrating this.*) Getting him back is the sort of thing that could give the nation hope again. Never underestimate the power of British pluck.

JOCK: And a cash reward.

COLONEL: Quite so.

(*DAPHNE enters.*)

Oh, I'm so sorry, I didn't realise you had company.

JOCK: Daphne's staying here for a few days, Colonel. I had reason to believe she was in grave danger. Daphne Fritters this is Colonel Gardener.

DAPHNE: We've met. I have already asked the Colonel's help in tracking down my father. Is there any news?

COLONEL: Good heavens, woman, I'm sure your father's perfectly safe. He left you a note didn't he? I haven't got time to waste on such things. One of our national treasures is missing. Good day to you both.

JOCK: Good day sir.

(*The COLONEL exits.*)

DAPHNE: That rude man. I shall have words with Papa about him. What did he mean about one of our national treasures?

JOCK: He means Mr Barton.

DAPHNE: Mr Barton was kidnapped during the burglary at Lady Laxington's.

JOCK: That wasn't Mr Barton. The real Dick Barton would never have let you down. That was his colourful working-class cockney sidekick Snowy White disguised as our boss. We got the idea of having him stand in after you mistook him for the governor on your first visit.

DAPHNE: Then Mr Barton is still in bed?

JOCK: I'm afraid that was another deception. You see he was never confined to the bedroom. We had to tell everyone that because he was away on a secret mission. Now with the master and Snowy gone nothing stands between us and the forces of EFIL.

DAPHNE: How can you say that when the free world has a guardian of such nobility, strength and down to earth homespun intelligence.

JOCK: And who might that be, lassie?

DAPHNE: Why you Jock.

JOCK: Och I'm not the dashing hero type.

DAPHNE: You've been my hero from that first night.

JOCK: What night?

DAPHNE: Don't tell me you didn't feel the enchantment too? (*Sings.*)

A Nightingale Sang in Berkley Square

THAT CERTAIN NIGHT, THE NIGHT WE MET,
THERE WAS MAGIC ABROAD IN THE AIR,
THERE WERE ANGELS DINING AT THE RITZ

JOCK: (*Sings.*)

AND A NIGHTINGALE SANG IN BERKLEY SQUARE
I MAY BE RIGHT, I MAY BE WRONG
BUT I'M PERFECTLY WILLING TO SWEAR
THAT WHEN YOU TURNED AND SMILED AT ME

DAPHNE: (*Sings.*)

A NIGHTINGALE SANG IN BERKLEY SQUARE.

JOCK: (*Sings.*)

THE MOON THAT LINGERED OVER LONDON TOWN
LAUGHED AT OUR LITTLE RENDEZVOUS,
HOW COULD A ROUGH AND READY LAD LIKE ME
BE TALKING WI' A LASS LIKE YOU?

DAPHNE: (*Sings.*)

YOUR WORDS ARE COARSE, YOUR ACCENT'S QUEER

JOCK/DAPHNE: (*Sing.*)

WE'RE A QUITE INCOMPATIBLE PAIR
BUT AS WE STOOD AND SAID GOODNIGHT
A NIGHTINGALE SANG IN BERKLEY SQUARE.

DAPHNE: (*Sings.*)

WHEN DAWN CAME STEALING WITH ITS GOLDEN CHARMS
I LONGED TO LINGER IN YOUR ARMS,
YOU TURNED AND SPOKE TO ME, THAT WAY YOU DO,
(*Scottish accent.*)
'YOU BONNY LASS, OCH AYE THE NOO!'

JOCK: (*Sings.*)

MY HOMEWARD STEP WAS JUST AS LIGHT

AS THE SHORTBREAD OF GRANNY MCNAIR,

AND LIKE AN ECHO FAR AWAY

JOCK/DAPHNE: (*Sing.*)

A NIGHTINGALE SANG IN BERKLEY SQUARE.

(*The tune is not resolved. The phone rings.*)
DAPHNE: Perhaps that's Mr Barton now.
(*JOCK answers the phone.*)
JOCK: It's for you.
(*DAPHNE takes the receiver.*)
DAPHNE: Daphne Fritters – I see, thank you Charlton.
(*She hangs up.*) That was our butler. He told me that
Father has sent a message urging me to send a trusty
friend with money and supplies to his hiding place in the
darkest East End.
JOCK: Fear not Daphne I shall be that trusty friend.
DAPHNE: Oh would you Jock. I'd go myself but you hear
such stories of the East End. Strong drink, loose morals
and jellied eels. Besides I'm a girl.
JOCK: Just leave everything to me. (*He puts on a Barton mac
and trilby.*) How do I look?
DAPHNE: My hero, every inch Dick Barton.
JOCK: No, no lassie from now on it's Rick Tartan.
DAPHNE: I'm the luckiest gal in the British Empire.
JOCK/DAPHNE: (*Sing.*)

THAT CERTAIN NIGHT, THE NIGHT WE MET,

THERE WAS MAGIC ABROAD IN THE AIR,

THERE WERE ANGELS DINING AT THE RITZ

AND A NIGHTINGALE SANG IN BERKLEY SQUARE

I KNOW 'CAUSE I WAS THERE

THAT NIGHT IN BERKLEY SQUARE –

BBC ANOUNCER: Meanwhile at The Viper's Nest, Snowy
has fallen under the influence of strong drink.

Scene 11

The Viper's Nest.

SNOWY: 'Ere. Give us another cuppa.

SCARHEART: No more tea until you've mastered your lines.

SNOWY: (*Like a desperate drug addict.*) Oh go on just one more, go on, just a little sip, I can handle it, I can honestly, I can, I could stop any time I wanted. In fact I'm thinking of kicking the habit after this next one. I've got to come off it slowly like.

SCARHEART: Not until you've rehearsed your wireless broadcast.

SNOWY: What broadcast, chief?

SCARHEART: Please concentrate. I'll go through this one more time. When the legions of EFIL ransack the country, you, Dick Barton, will make a broadcast to the nation.

SNOWY: And I keep telling you, I'm not Dick Barton.

SCARHEART: Oh really? And who are you then?

SNOWY: I don't know, maybe another cup of char might refresh my memory.

SCARHEART: When you've rehearsed the broadcast.

SNOWY: Give it 'ere. (*SNOWY looks over the script.*) I can't say this. It ain't natural. You can tell it's been written by a foreigner.

SCARHEART: (*Exasperated.*) Very well, in your own words.

SNOWY: (*As if broadcasting.*) Watch'a mateys, it's your old mucker Dicky Barton 'ere. How you diddling? 'Ere, I'll tell you what though, if you should notice foreign johnnies in jackboots marching through your back yard, take no notice, they're only 'avin a laugh. You gotta laugh, aint you? That's what I say. (*Sings.*) 'When you're smilin', when you're smilin' – ' (*SCARHEART clips the back of his head.*) Anyway, toodle-pip treakles and have another cuppa on your old guv'nor Mrs Barton's boy, Ricky.

SCARHEART: Good God. I always knew British Intelligence was a contradiction in terms.

SNOWY: Oxymoron.

SCARHEART: That's quite enough from you! Now if we only knew the whereabouts of the rest of the tea supplies. (*A CRIMINAL rushes in.*)

CRIMINAL: We've found the Minister of Rationing.

SCARHEART: Sir Stanley Fritters? Where is he?

CRIMINAL: His butler Charlton's a recent convert to EFIL. He says Fritters is holed up at Fishfinger Wharf in Wapping. But he's a tough one. Charlton don't reckon he'll crack.

SCARHEART: You underestimate me. I perfected my innate wolf cruelty on the smaller boarders at Eton. He'll snap as easily as Riddlington-Smythe Minor on the third day of Michaelmas term. The secret is to threaten the teddy bear.

CRIMINAL: We've discovered his daughter's hiding out at Dick Barton's HQ.

SCARHEART: Almost as good. Have her brought here to The Viper's Nest. I'm off to Fishfinger Wharf.

CRIMINAL: (*Of SNOWY.*) What shall I do with him?

SCARHEART: Lock him in that old shack down by the railway track. (*He sweeps out.*)

SNOWY: 'Ere matey you've got a kind face. Spare us a cuppa tea.
(*MARTA bursts in.*)

MARTA: Where is he? Where is my darling?

CRIMINAL: Evening Miss Heartburn.

SNOWY: Alright treacle? You're in a bit of a mither aint you?

MARTA: My angel, we are reunited. (*She picks SNOWY up and snogs him hard.*)

SNOWY: (*Recovering.*) Lor, love a duck!

MARTA: It's not him.

CRIMINAL: What?

MARTA: That's not him. It's not Dick Barton.

CRIMINAL: How can you tell?

MARTA: Barton is a master lover, this is the kiss of a talentless peasant. (*She snogs SNOWY again.*) Ugh!

CRIMINAL: Are you sure?

MARTA: Well, you try.

(She pushes them together. They snog and part.)

Did his tongue pulsate inside you with the intensity of a lightning flash over a Bavarian lake at midnight?

CRIMINAL: No. I see what you mean.

MARTA: This is an imposter. I must find my beloved. I must find Dick Barton. *(She exits.)*

SNOWY: I kept telling everyone I wasn't 'im.

CRIMINAL: You'd better start saying your prayers whoever you are.

SNOWY: What are you going to do with me?

CRIMINAL: That will be for the Baron to decide. Meanwhile, you'll cool your heels down by the railway. With no tea.

SNOWY: *(Terrified.)* No, you've got to give me tea, I need it, I need me Rosie Lee.

CRIMINAL: I don't think so my unlucky friend. It's trainspotting time for you.

BBC ANOUNCER: Meanwhile, it's nearly midnight with not a sign of – Barton. Britain's hopes rest with a new hero – Rick Tartan, Special Agent. But things are not going well for the Scotch sleuth as he wanders lost in the desolate maze of London's docklands

Scene 12

Fishfinger Wharf.

JOCK enters in darkness shining his torch around. The sound of seagulls.

JOCK: Och! The smell of fish down here is something terrible. I've got to find Fishfinger Wharf, my wee lassie's depending on me. What have we here? Haddock Wharf, Cod Wharf, Fishfinger – ah ha! Sir Stanley are you there? Are you there, sir? Your daughter Daphne sent me. I've got some money, some clean underwear and this week's Eagle Comic.

(MARTA steps out of the shadows.)

MARTA: You're too late my love. The Baron and his friends have already made a house call. Sir Stanley Fritters is safely in the clutches of EFIL and soon you will be safely back in my arms where you belong. Did you think you could escape from your Marta? My darling, what we had was so special. I would track you down to the ends of the earth just for one of your sizzling kisses. Come to me my angel, kiss me! (*She sweeps him into snog. Comes up for air.*) Just a minute there's something wrong. (*Kisses him again.*) You're not Barton. Another imposter.
(*The COLONEL steps out of the shadows with a gun.*)

COLONEL: Raise your beautiful hands above your gorgeous head, Marta Heartburn. You're a prisoner of His Majesty's government.

MARTA: Colonel Gardener is it not? You were not so big and fierce with me on your last visit to Berlin.

COLONEL: I was a callow and impressionable young secret agent, damn you. You took advantage of me.

MARTA: Yes and so often.

COLONEL: British Intelligence paid dearly for the information you bullied from me. We've wanted to put you out of action for a very long time.

JOCK: But we're too late to save the minister, Colonel. Baron Scarheart got here before us and has taken him prisoner.

COLONEL: Heaven only knows what foul torture he's being subjected to.

MARTA: I could give you a little demonstration.

COLONEL: Silence. That's enough from you. (*To JOCK.*)
I would have got here sooner but my office is under siege.

JOCK: A foreign invasion?

COLONEL: Very far from it. An invasion of Dick Bartons.

MARTA: What!

COLONEL: Since the offer of a reward for his return appeared in this morning's *Times* there has been a queue of archetypal Englishman all the way along Whitehall, all claiming to be Dick Barton. What's so difficult is that everyone knows so much about him from the radio serials. It's impossible to pick out the imposters from questioning them.

MARTA: I could tell you.

COLONEL: You? What do you know of our man?

MARTA: I consumed every inch of him every hour for over three weeks. His kiss is like nothing on earth. I would know it anywhere.

COLONEL: But great heavens woman there must be five hundred men queuing up outside my office. You can't make love to every one of them.

MARTA: Watch me.

(*MARTA and the the COLONEL go. JOCK is about follow.*)

JOCK: But what's this? One of the villains has dropped a book of matches – and there's writing on it. 'The Viper's Nest'. Don't worry Daphne. I'm on my way.

(*JOCK rushes off.*)

BBC ANOUNCER: Meanwhile in Whitehall, the tireless search for the real Dick Barton continues unabated.

Scene 13

Whitehall.

MARTA: How many Dicks have I kissed now Colonel?

COLONEL : That was number 563. I must say for a foreign lass you've got extraordinary stamina. Your unique talents have caught the intention of the entire Whitehall staff. Carry on like this and there'll be an invitation to the war office Christmas party for you.

MARTA: It is not for your crummy approbation that I conduct my tireless search. It is my heart, my heart which yearns for the man I love.

COLONEL: Jolly good show. Can I offer you a sandwich?

MARTA: We must carry on, carry on you understand?

COLONEL: But your beautiful lips must need refreshment.

MARTA: I am made of sterner stuff. Have you not heard of my tireless work entertaining the troops? I just have to give, give, give.

COLONEL: I quite understand. Vera Lynn's exactly the same. (*Beat.*) I must say I'm still nervous about our rejecting candidate 278. He was an old Etonian.

MARTA: He also had a wooden leg, a lisp, a metal plate in his head and one arm was longer then the other.

COLONEL: But in an emergency under dim lighting conditions?

MARTA: No one, no one can take the place of the genuine Dick Barton.

COLONEL: I suppose not. Well I think there's time for one more before lunch. Let's have him in. (*Into the phone.*) Thank you Pixie.

(*A CANDIDATE enters, played by the DICK BARTON actor, who not surprisingly looks exactly like DICK BARTON. MARTA and the COLONEL gasp.*)

COLONEL: It looks like…It looks like…I think…I think…

MARTA: At last this could be the real thing.

COLONEL: Well stop wasting time, woman. Kiss him and lets find out.

(*MARTA kisses the CANDIDATE passionately. She surfaces.*)

COLONEL: Well, is this the real Dick Barton?

MARTA: I don't know it's not quite as I remember but yes! Yes I think it is!

COLONEL: Welcome back to the fold old boy.

(*The CANDIDATE speaks for the first time. Unfortunately he has a thick Birmingham accent and is blatantly not DICK BARTON.*)

CANDIDATE: Oooh er, thanks Bab. I can't wait to do all them secret agent type things. But I'll have to pop back to Bromsgrove to see if the missus can feed me pigeons.

MARTA: No, foiled again! Will this torture never end?

COLONEL: (*To the CANDIDATE.*) Get out you cowardly impostor and be grateful we don't set the dogs on you.

CANDIDATE: Very sorry I'm sure. (*He exits.*)

MARTA: I can't stand it any more. To be so close and yet to have my hopes smashed into a thousand pieces. Why! Why has fate done this to me!?

(*DICK BARTON himself walks in.*)

DICK BARTON: Ah good afternoon, everyone, Barton here reporting for duty. Good to see you're batting for our team now Marta.

MARTA: GET OUT! GET OUT you cruel impostor can't you see my heart is breaking and yet you and your countrymen come here to taunt me with your phoney accent, dashing mackintosh and natty little hat perched at a rakish angle. No more Colonel, I beg you, I can't stand it, my heart is breaking. Don't make me carry on. (*We see RODGER and WILCO, the gay secret agents, behind enemy lines. They are bluff, butch and public school even though they call each other darling.*)

RODGER/WILCO: Calling London HQ! Calling London HQ! Attention London. We have red alert.

RODGER: Secret agents Rodger and Wilco here.

WILCO: Partners in spying –

RODGER: – And show-tune aficionados. Wilco's just been terribly brave. Haven't you, darling?

WILCO: All in the call of duty, Rodge.

RODGER: Late last night Wilco penetrated a terrorist ring.

WILCO: You would have done the same, darling.

RODGER: It seems the blighters have placed a bomb in Whitehall HQ. There's enough explosives there to play havoc with the soft furnishings.

WILCO: I must say I won't be sorry to see that carpet go.

RODGER: The bomb is primed for 1.00pm Greenwich Mean Time and set to detonate at any use of cheap sexual innuendo. It's vital that you avoid any use of smut during the lunch hour. You must evacuate!

WILCO: Repeat – evacuate!

RODGER: Repeat – evacuate!!!

WILCO: You can be awfully commanding Rodgina.

RODGER: Thanks Wiggy!

BOTH: This is Rodger and Wilco.

WILCO: Saying over –

BOTH: – And out.
(*Back to Whitehall.*)

COLONEL: But Miss Heartburn take courage, it's lunch hour. Just one more time and then you can have a nice rest.

MARTA: I won't do it.

COLONEL: You must do it. The future of the free world could depend on it. You must carry on.

MARTA: You can beg, plead and barter all you like but I will not put my lips on your doppelganger!

(*A huge explosion. Black out. Lights up on MARTA lying amongst bomb debris.*)

DICK BARTON: Don't worry, I'm a trained life saver. (*Gives her the kiss of life.*)

MARTA: (*Recovers.*) My hero!

DICK BARTON: Pardon me ma'am, I must go. Duty calls. The survival of the free world is in my hands. (*He exits.*)

MARTA: (*Stunned, stares after him.*) That was the real Dick Barton!

BBC ANOUNCER: And indeed it was. Meanwhile at The Viper's Nest, Sir Stanley Fritters, fearful for his daughter's life has revealed his secrets to Baron Scarheart. Are the exertions of EFIL to prove unstoppable?

Scene 14

The Viper's Nest.

SIR STANLEY: I've told you the location of Britain's tea supplies, now let my daughter and I go.

SCARHEART: Oh no. Just as we were getting to know one another. Can't we play a little longer?

SIR STANLEY: What do you mean, you devil?

SCARHEART: Thanks to your information my legions are at this moment standing by at tea warehouses all over the nation. They wait for the stroke of Big Ben at midnight to sound across the wireless waves on the chill night air. At this pre-arranged signal they will contaminate the nation's lifeblood with Slunk. Within days, Britain's brains will be an unresponsive mush ready to receive the imprint of EFIL's jackboot. So now you and your precious daughter have become expendable – and there's nothing I enjoy more than expending.

SIR STANLEY: My daughter is an innocent child.

SCARHEART: Oh dear. Life can be so cruel, can't it? (*A CRIMINAL rushes in pushing JOCK.*)

CRIMINAL: Baron, Baron we caught this one!

JOCK: Scarheart, I knew you couldn't be far away, I detected the stench of EFIL.

SCARHEART: That aroma is the sweet smell of victory my friend, victory for me and all EFIL kind.

JOCK: Never. While Dick Barton lives and breathes.

SCARHEART: Ah, but does he? (*The CRIMINAL ties JOCK to a chair alongside SIR STANLEY.*) Where is the noble and upright guardian of all that's good, wholesome and squeaky clean? The free world waits in vain for Barton.

JOCK: You won't be laughing when he gets back.

SCARHEART: Bring in the girl too. (*CRIMINAL exits.*) Add her charming face to this pretty posy of righteousness.

SIR STANLEY: You'll pay for this you blasted foreigner. In this world or the next.

SCARHEART: It is you Fritters, you and your shabby friends who have a one-way ticket to the next world and guess what? It's nearly take off time. (*DAPHNE is brought in.*)

DAPHNE: Unhand me you brute. (*She struggles. The CRIMINAL swears in a foreign language and exits.*)

SIR STANLEY: Steady, Daphne. Let's not show these johnny foreigners that we're afraid of them. Their strange unnatural accents have no hold on our hearts.

JOCK: I beg your pardon?

DAPHNE: Don't worry Jock, Daddy doesn't mean you.

SCARHEART: Is everybody listening?

SIR STANLEY: Spit your worst. We shall soothe the venom from your viperous tongue with the strains of rousing anthems from our glorious past. Come, Daphne, 'Land of Hope and Glory' if you please. (*He starts to hum.*)

DAPHNE: Do you know this one at all, Jock?

JOCK: I think so, lassie.

DAPHNE: All together now –

(*They hum defiantly under the following.*)

SCARHEART: At 23.45 a mechanism will release a greased cannonball along a metal groove fiendishly fashioned for this very purpose. As it reaches the end it will drop from a height of 23 feet onto the raised portion of a child's seesaw, catapulting a Swiss cheese into the air. It will land on the stone floor beneath causing it to break open and release an aroma that will attract vermin from the surrounding area. The ravenous creatures will pour into the chamber causing the minutely controlled temperature to rise. This slight increase will trigger a spring mechanism tipping over the tank above your heads. (*They stop singing and look up.*)

Contained in that tank are three gallons of rancid honey imported specially for the occasion from the forests of Bavaria. The sickly mixture will tip down, coating you from head to foot in syrup. Excess of this will seep beneath the floorboards where an army of Namibian blood-sucking killer ants are currently dozing. The ants will swarm up through the floor attracted by the honey and slowly suck out your blood. Meanwhile, your every nerve-ending will be tortured by a million, trillion little feet scrabbling across your skin, up your nose, in your mouth and eye sockets and into little crevices you never even dreamt you had.

SIR STANLEY: A terrible agonising death. What kind of a mind could concoct such a horror?

SCARHEART: Oh there's plenty more where that came from. We had to make our own entertainment in the wolf pack. Well, I'd love to stay and watch but I've got a bit of a tea party to plan. The door will seal behind me. The only way out is through the killer ants. Have fun, sleep tight and make sure the bugs don't bite. (*He exits.*)

DAPHNE: What ever shall we do?

SIR STANLEY: It would seem we're doomed.

JOCK: Don't despair missy. Dick Barton will save us.

DAPHNE: But where is he?

JOCK: He'd want us to be strong. He'd want us to remember the motto of the Bartons.

SIR STANLEY: 'The Motto of The Bartons'. That sounds like just the ticket. How does it go?

JOCK: (*Sings, unaccompanied.*)

THE MOTTO OF THE BARTONS

IS GIVE EACH JOB YOUR BEST.

KEEP A STIFF UPPER LIP

AND ALWAYS WEAR A VEST.

(*From the cellar beneath we hear DICK's echoing voice completing the chorus.*)

DICK BARTON: (*Voice below.*)

PACK A TOOTHBRUSH

AND CHANGE YOUR UNDERWEAR,

EAT AN APPLE EVERY DAY

AND COMB YOUR HAIR.

SIR STANLEY: What's that?

DAPHNE: It sounds like it's coming from the cellar.

(*DICK BARTON pops his head up through the trap door.*)

DICK BARTON: (*Sings.*)

HAIL DICK BARTON, HE'S AWF'LLY, AWF'LLY BRAVE

(*EVERYONE joins in.*)

BRITONS NEVER, NEVER, NEVER

SHALL BE SLAVES!

JOCK: DB! I knew you wouldn't let us down. What kept you, sir?

(*DICK BARTON speaks to them with his head sticking out of the trap door.*)

DICK BARTON: Sorry about the delay everyone. After I escaped Marta Heartburn's clutches I had many, many adventures on my way home. I had to organise a great escape from Colditz, bust a few damns and lead an Austrian family with a singing nun across the Alps but I'm here now. (*Struck by a sudden strange sensation.*) My goodness!

JOCK: What's the matter chief?

DICK BARTON: Avert your eyes, miss, I fear I'm going to have to scratch myself in a private place.

DAPHNE: It's the ants.

SIR STANLEY: A few of the pluckier fellows may have climbed your trouser leg.

(*DICK BARTON scrambles out of the trap door and examines an ant from his shoe.*)

DICK BARTON: Good God! Namibian blood-sucking killer ants.

DAPHNE: And the cellar's full of them.

JOCK: The only way out is right through them.

(*Ant noises up through the trap door.*)

DICK BARTON: The little blighters are waking up. I must have disturbed them.

DAPHNE: Scarheart's arranged we'll be coated in honey at any moment.

DICK BARTON: That'll drive 'em crazy. The devil.

SIR STANLEY: Even you can't save us now Barton.

DICK BARTON: We're not beaten yet. Let's see what I have here. (*He starts to go through his pockets.*) Clean underwear. We could make a sling from the knickers' elastic and then...No. Toothbrush! We could brush them away with frantic little sweeping motions...No. A box of drawing pins. They're no use...Wait a minute...It might just work...Each one of you take four drawing pins and push one into the sole of your shoe at each heel and toe.

SIR STANLEY: What good will that do?

DICK BARTON: Quickly sir, there's no time to lose.

JOCK: What are we going to do DB?

DICK BARTON: There's only one thing guaranteed to make Namibian blood-sucker killer ants scarper and that's the sound of approaching elephants.

DAPHNE: Where are we going to get elephants at this hour Mr Barton?

DICK BARTON: We won't have to. We're going to trick the little blighters into thinking there's a herd approaching.

SIR STANLEY: How do we do that?

DICK BARTON: We tap.

THE OTHERS: What!?

DICK BARTON: Watch me. It's just a simple three step, shuffle, ball change combination but it could save the free world. (*Sings, demonstrating.*)

Happy Feet

HAPPY FEET.

I'VE GOT THOSE HAPPY FEET

GIVE THEM A LOW DOWN BEAT

AND THEY BEGIN DANCING

(*DAPHNE gives it a try.*)

DAPHNE: (*Sings.*)

I'VE GOT THOSE

TEN LITTLE TAPPING TOES

AND WHEN I HEAR A TUNE

I CAN'T CONTROL

MY DANCING FEET TO SAVE MY SOUL

(*JOCK's turn.*)

JOCK: (*Sings.*)

WEARY BLUES

DON'T GET INTO MY SHOES

BECAUSE MY SHOES REFUSE

TO EVER GROW WEARY

DAPHNE: (*Spoken.*) Come on, Father.

SIR STANLEY: (*Sings. Somewhat reluctantly.*)

I KEEP CHEERFUL ON AN EARFUL OF MUSIC STREET

I'VE GOT THOSE

HAP-HAP-HAPPY FEET

(*They ALL do a step combination.*)

DAPHNE: Is it working?

(*DICK BARTON looks down into the cellar.*)

DICK BARTON: The ants are dispersing. Come on everyone let's tap for victory.

(*They do a frantic, elaborate silly tap routine together. JOCK looks down into the trap.*)

JOCK: The ants are dispersing DB.

DICK BARTON: Quickly everyone down through the cellar. But for heaven's sake keep tapping.

(*Off they go. The BBC ANNOUNCER tap dances on the spot as he says:*)

BBC ANOUNCER: And so Dick Barton rescues Sir Stanley, Daphne and Jock from the Baron's vile trap. As swiftly as a speeding bullet, Barton makes his way to Big Ben with midnight fast approaching. An army of wolves guard the entrance. Proof if proof were needed that Scarheart is standing, gloating high above London's streets, ready to savour his moment of triumph from Big Ben itself.

Scene 15

Big Ben.

SCARHEART on the parapet of Big Ben in front of the clock face. Big Ben tolls quarter to midnight. A clap of thunder. Wolves howl.

SCARHEART: Sing, sing to the blood red harvest moon my sharp-fanged angels of the night. Soon all of Britain will tremble at our feeding frenzy. In a few moments, midnight will toll throughout this mean-spirited, damp little island, heralding a new dawn of EFIL.

MARTA: (*Approaching.*) Otto! Are you there?

SCARHEART: Marta! Out here my angel of darkness, out here amongst the stars surveying our kingdom.

(*MARTA joins him on the parapet.*)

Is this not a beautiful sight?

MARTA: I have no time to wallow in your victory. I am on a mission of the heart.

SCARHEART: Of the heart my dearest?

MARTA: Is there not an emptiness in your soul? An emptiness where love should be?

SCARHEART: Now you come to mention it…No. What kind of a man can have captured your heart?

MARTA: A god amongst men. Once I feared him as every creature of darkness fears him but now I yearn for his lips.

SCARHEART: Who? Who can you mean?

MARTA: My heart belongs to Dick Barton.

SCARHEART: Dick Barton! You bring shame upon the name of EFIL.

MARTA: If I could only reach him I know I could persuade him to hang up the trilby of truth and don the mackintosh of the merciless...

SCARHEART: I doubt if any woman alive has such power.

MARTA: But I must try. I know he will come here tonight. Keep watch for me here and I shall look out over the Thames from the other side. (*She moves out of sight around the tower.*)

SCARHEART: Please yourself. Two minutes left, two minutes to the greatest moment of my gloriously despicable life. (*SNOWY now looking exactly like DICK BARTON appears with a gun.*)

SNOWY: Hands up Scarheart. You're under arrest.

SCARHEART: Barton!

SNOWY: No, it's me Snowy. And I'll have no more of your drugs, it was tough going but I went cold spam and got clean of 'em. Now, with the governor unable to stop you. I reckon he'd want me to step in and be the bleedin 'ero.

SCARHEART: How did you get past the wolves?

SNOWY: That was no problem for me. My old man used to work in the wolf house at London zoo. I was brought up with 'em. I know their ways, you've got to respect them. A wolf ate my little brother.

SCARHEART: What nonsense.

SNOWY: Oh yeh, my dad took me and my brother on a wolf-catching trip to Bavaria only me brother wandered off. We searched everywhere but all we found was his teddy bear.

SCARHEART: What did this bear look like?

SNOWY: I always carry 'im with me. 'Ere you are. (*To the*

bear.) Say hello to the nasty foreign bloke.

SCARHEART: But that's Boboo! I'd know him anywhere. I lost that bear the day the wolves found me...Boboo! Come to my arms. (*Snatches the bear.*) At last we are reunited. (*To SNOWY.*) But just a minute, your brother you say...? But that means...

SNOWY: 'Ere, give us that bear back.

(*SCARHEART doesn't.*)

SCARHEART: Never. The bonds of boy and bear are as strong as the bonds of blood. You don't know how long I have dreamt of this meeting. I want you to join me in my crusade.

SNOWY: Well that depends.

SCARHEART: Depends?

SNOWY: Well, Mr Barton pays me two bob an hour. How much could you pay?

SCARHEART: Three and a half.

SNOWY: Plus ten bob for the teddy?

SCARHEART: Seven and a half.

SNOWY: When do I start?

SCARHEART: My brother in EFIL! Start immediately. Midnight approaches as does the zenith of my plan. There is one who has betrayed our cause. She must not be allowed to disrupt the onward march of EFIL. You will find her on the other side of this tower looking out over the river. Kill her and toss her broken body over the parapet.

SNOWY: (*Chirpy.*) Right you are chief. Anything else? Just say the word. Three and a half shillings an hour, cor blimey. (*He goes off after MARTA.*)

SCARHEART: Mother, now I know you're out there somewhere watching over me. Thirty seconds until midnight. Sleep on, England. Sleep on, the rich man in his castle, the crofter in his humble cottage, the shopkeepers and the serving maid, the farmer and the engineer.

(*Thunder and lightning.*)

Sleep deep in the comfort of innocence. You will need all your strength for the horrors of the morn. Ten, nine, eight, seven, six, five, four, three, two.

(*Bang! A gun shot. SCARHEART falls onto the minute hand of Big Ben jamming it and stopping it reaching twelve. DICK BARTON appears.*)

I promised you three and six an hour. Judas!

DICK BARTON: Barton, actually Dick Barton. Snowy told me you were out here. You didn't really believe that he would turn to EFIL did you? His father *did* work for the wolf house at London zoo but you fell for one of the oldest tricks in the book. Secret Agent Boboo report back to HQ. Your work here is done.

(*The TEDDY exits 'sooty'-like.*)

(*Calls off.*) Snowy, guard the entrance to the tower, there's a good chap. (*To SCARHEART.*) Sorry I had to shoot you old boy but I had to find some way of jamming the clock and stopping it striking midnight.

SCARHEART: With my dying breath I curse you Barton.

(*SCARHEART dies.*)

DICK BARTON: God rest his soul. He's with some power of goodness now. May the angels save him.

(*SIR STANLEY appears.*)

SIR STANLEY: Good God, that's a lot of stairs. Are you alright Barton?

DICK BARTON: Perfectly thank you sir.

SIR STANLEY: It would seem you've done it again. Saved the day and thwarted EFIL.

DICK BARTON: Yes, it does rather look that way doesn't it. How did you get into the tower?

SIR STANLEY: Snowy helped us through the wolves. He's quite something with those animals isn't he?

DICK BARTON: That's the working class in him I expect. Marvellous affinity with animals they have.

SIR STANLEY: He's teaching Daphne how to make them sit up and shake paws.

(*JOCK appears.*)

JOCK: DB are you alright? We got here as fast as we could.

DICK BARTON: I'm sure you did Jock old boy.

SIR STANLEY: The twinkling lights of London look beautiful beneath us. A treasure that every man, woman and child in this blessed nation of ours can enjoy. Spread out like a cascade of precious jewels adrift on a black velvet sea.

DICK BARTON: Pray God that foreign hands never reach out and grab our baubles.

SIR STANLEY: I feel sure that the world's EFIL forces will be defeated soon. (*Slaps JOCK on the back.*) If you and your trusty comrades have anything to do with it.

JOCK: (*Plucks up the courage.*) Sir Stanley, may I have permission to marry your daughter.

SIR STANLEY: (*Casually.*) Don't be silly, you're too common.

JOCK: Oh yes, sorry I forgot.

SIR STANLEY: Get some of this down you, Barton. I've brought a flask of uncontaminated tea. I thought we could all probably do with a pick-me-up.

DICK BARTON: Righty-oh, sir and then it's back to HQ for us.

(*ALL drink from the flask. MARTA arrives brandishing a gun.*)

MARTA: Not so fast my love. I have searched for you all over London. Too many times you have slipped from my arms but no longer. To every side of you is a 300 foot drop. Before you is a W. H. Smith and Weston 56 colt pistol. The deluxe model with self-cleaning barrel and optional holster trim. A deadly weapon of destruction guaranteed to be mercilessly accurate in my beautiful hands and devastating on impact. Nothing can save you now except the love of a cruel and wicked woman. A woman who longs for your lips. A woman who would kill rather than lose you to another. Pledge your heart to me my love, renounce goodness and convert to EFIL or you and your friends will never see the dawn.

JOCK: Oh no! Boss, what are you going to do?

SIR STANLEY: Yes Barton. I'd give my eye teeth to know how you're going to get out of this one.

DICK BARTON: Well, there's only one sure way to find out?

JOCK/SIR STANLEY: What's that?

BBC ANNOUNCER: Tune in to the next exciting instalment of –

EVERYONE: Dick Barton – Special Agent!

(*Dick Barton theme.*)

The End.

DICK BARTON AND THE CURSE
OF THE PHARAOH'S TOMB

Characters

DICK BARTON

KING GEORGE VI

JOCK

FIRST MUMMY
at the Colony Rooms and Buckingham Palace

HUGO 'SWANKER' WHITE
an Archaeologist

THE VIZIER

M.C.
at The Needle's Eye

MARTA HEARTBURN

QUEEN NEFATARTIE

MURIEL BELCHER

BBC ANNOUNCER

SNOWY

JULIAN 'PIGGY' PETHRINGTON
an archaeologist

PHARAOH AHKAN RAH

MRS HORROCKS

SECOND MUMMY
at Big Ben and Colossus' Tomb

RODGER
a secret agent

WILCO
a secret agent

Dick Barton and the Curse of the Pharaoh's Tomb was was commissioned by the Warehouse Theatre Company and first performed at the Warehouse Theatre, Croydon, on Friday 10 December 1999, with the following cast:

DICK BARTON/KING GEORGE VI, Clive Carter

MARTA/NEFATARTIE/MURIEL, Sophie-Louise Dann

PIGGY/AHKAN RAH, Mark Roper

SWANKER/VIZIER/M.C., Duncan Wisbey

JOCK/MUMMY, Darrell Brockis

BBC ANNOUNCER/SNOWY, William Oxborrow

Other characters played by members of the cast

Director, Ted Craig

Designer, Stuart Stanley

Musical Director, Stefan Bednarczyk

Lighting, Douglas Kuhrt

Costumes, Andri Korniotis

It is strongly suggested that the principle roles are doubled as in the original production.

This text went to press before the opening night, and may therefore differ slightly from the text as performed.

MUSICAL NUMBERS

All lyrics by Phil Willmott

ACT ONE

THREE LITTLE ARCHEOLOGISTS
Music: 'Three Little Maids From School' by Sullivan
Dick Barton, Piggy & Swanker

THE LEGEND OF AHKAN RAH
Music: 'Marche Slave' by Tchaikovsky
Dick Barton (with interjection from Jock)

SINGLE PHARAOH SEEKS A GIRLFRIEND
Music: 'Dance Of The Flutes', from 'The Nutcracker'
by Tchaikovsky
Ahkan Rah

TALENT
Music: variations on 'Then One Of Us Will Be The
Queen', from 'The Gondoliers' by Sullivan
Nefatartie

THE PROPOSAL
Music: quick burst of 'Nessun Dorma' by Puccini
Ahkan Rah

THINKING BIG/ONE HUNDRED NIGHTS
Music: a medley of waltzes, 'Vienna Blood' & 'Artist's
Life' by Strauss
Nefatartie/Ahkan Rah

PIGGY'S PRAYER
Music: variations on 'Toccata and Fugue' by Bach
Piggy

ACT TWO

THE PHARAOH RAG
Music: variations on the main theme of 'Swan Lake' by Tchaikovsky
Nefatartie, King George VI, Piggy & Company

THINKING BIG (REPRISE.)
Music: 'Vienna Blood' by Strauss
Nefatartie

THE FISH SONG
Music: Ben Glay Bay, Trad. Scottish folk song
Dick Barton (with interjection from Jock)

A RHYME FOR MURIAL
Music: main theme from overture to the 'Barber of Seville' by Rossini
Swanker

OUT OF THE PAST
Music: 'Oh My Beloved Father' by Puccini
Nefatartie

BARTON IS YOUR MAN
Music: medley of 'The Sailor's Horn Pipe', 'A Life On The Ocean Wave', 'What Shall We Do With The Drunken Sailor'
Dick Barton, Jock, Swanker and BBC Announcer

ACT ONE

BBC ANNOUNCER: This is the BBC from London. It's 6.45 and time for the next exciting instalment of Dick Barton – Special Agent.

(*We hear the Dick Barton theme tune* – The Devil's Gallop.)

In the last episode our hero was trapped at the top of Big Ben by the evil temptress Marta Heartburn. The ruthless harridan has fallen for the wholesome, clean-cut charms of our hero and her chilling ultimatum rings out through the cold night air.

(*Lights up on MARTA holding DICK BARTON and JOCK at gunpoint at the top of Big Ben.*)

MARTA: Renounce the trilby of truth and don the mackintosh of the merciless or prepare to die. To every side of you is a 300 foot drop. In my hand is a W. H. Smith and Weston 56 colt revolver. The deluxe model with self-cleaning barrel and optional holster trim. Convert to EFIL or I pull the trigger and dispatch its deadly contents deep into the hearts of you and your colourful working-class assistants. What's it to be Barton – death or take the initials E.F.I.L. as your own?

DICK BARTON: The society of Evil Foreigners in London will never count Jock, Snowy and myself amongst its brood. I know I speak for us all in choosing an honourable death for king and country – eh lads?

JOCK: Och DB! Let's not do anything hasty here. Snowy's got a doctor's appointment in the morning and you know how cross they get if you don't turn up.

DICK BARTON: You're right old chap, there's the credibility of our fledgling National Health Service to be taken into account.

JOCK: It'll be the envy of the world DB.

DICK BARTON: Quite right. (*Refering to MARTA.*) How like a foreigner to try and undermine it. You give me no option but to pledge my life to EFIL – oh no...hold on a minute.

(*MARTA lets her coat fall to the floor revealing her fabulous body.*)

JOCK: She has kept herself awfully trim, boss.

(*DICK BARTON is apparently staring at her cleavage.*)

DICK BARTON: Good God! How magnificent.

MARTA: Ah ha! No man alive can resist me.

DICK BARTON: (*Still staring at her.*) Where did you get that?

MARTA: (*Rather mystified.*) They came as a pair.

DICK BARTON: Not those. The sapphire you wear around your neck it's...

MARTA: I stole it from an admirer. An eminent archaeologist I lured to my web.

DICK BARTON: Good grief, not Hugo 'Swanker' White?

MARTA: A stubborn man but he learnt that Marta always gets what she wants.

DICK BARTON: I'm not surprised he was stubborn. Do you know what you have around your neck? That's one of the three stones of Ahkan Rah!

MARTA: He called out that name as I trampled his broken heart into the dust. But what of this? The dawn is breaking. Proclaim your love for me across the rooftops of London or prepare to die.

DICK BARTON: Good gracious! You're right, the dawn! You don't know how much danger you're in. Cast the sapphire into some dark place before it is touched by the rays of the rising sun.

MARTA: Throw away my precious? Are you mad?

DICK BARTON: The stone is cursed. It was stolen from the tomb of Ahkan Rah. The curse states that should the dawn ever illuminate its cold beauty then a great evil will be released to seek a terrible revenge on the desecrators of the tomb.

MARTA: What has that to do with me?

DICK BARTON: And the bearer of the jewel will die.

MARTA: (*Momentarily worried.*) Ah. (*Dismissive again.*) Pah! Do you think I am frightened of such fairy stories? What place is there for such superstitious nonsense in this modern world of Bakelite?

DICK BARTON: Marta. The sun is rising. I beg you to cover up that sapphire.

MARTA: Never, I could no more hide the jewel then suppress my love for you.

DICK BARTON: Marta, the sapphire!

(*A clap of thunder. The sun rises. Music. A deep disembodied voice rumbles.*)

VOICE: AHKAN RAH!

(*For a second a flash of lightning throws a huge silhouette of the MUMMY onto them. MARTA screams and falls into DICK BARTON's arms as the lights restore to normal.*)

JOCK: Great heavens DB. Is she…is she…?

DICK BARTON: I'm afraid so. The deadly curse of the Pharaoh's Tomb has claimed its latest victim. Remove the sapphire for safe-keeping.

(*JOCK does so.*)

JOCK: DB look, there's some strange marking on her forehead.

DICK BARTON: So there is. It's a hieroglyph written in a secret burial script of the high priests of Ahkan Rah. An ancient language known to only a handful of eminent scholars. What words are hidden in those twisted symbols do you suppose?

JOCK: Now let's see – the little birdie means…and the water lily with three petals…I'm not an expert DB but I think it says – (*Harsh Arabic-sounding gobbledygook.*) Ahkland fad rast at clforkning safta karla ha.

DICK BARTON: Good gracious. You've studied the ancient lost burial language of Ahkan Rah?

JOCK: To be honest I wanted to do woodwork but it was the only evening class with a place left.

DICK BARTON: What does it mean, then?

JOCK: Well, roughly translated it means, and as I say I'm no expert…

DICK BARTON: Quickly man. The survival of the free world could depend on this.

JOCK: Well, it seems to say (*Pause, then with reverent wonder.*) – 'Mummy knows best'.

BBC ANNOUNCER: And so with these prophetic words resounding in their ears Dick and Jock carry the lovely form of spy Marta Heartburn to Barton's car. The trusty Bentley wends its way through London's streets as a grateful nation wakes to another day free from the tyranny of EFIL.

(*DICK BARTON and JOCK sitting in the front seats of the Bentley.*)

DICK BARTON: Do you think Snowy minded taking the bus with his cock-er-ny chums, Jock?

JOCK: I'm sure he didn't Boss.

DICK BARTON: He will insist on eating those whelks on the back seat and the vinegar stains the upholstery. Nasty rash he's getting on his face.

JOCK: He thinks it's all that dodgy tea he drank on our last adventure. All the tannin's given him a rotten outbreak of pimples.

DICK BARTON: The man's a martyr to the cause of British fair play.

JOCK: Talking of martyrs. Where are we taking the still lovely corpse of Marta Heartburn?

DICK BARTON: Yes, thank you Jock, I'll do the clever word play round here.

JOCK: Right you are DB.

DICK BARTON: We're off to the Egyptology department of the British Museum and my old friend Julian 'Piggy' Petherington. His very existence is under threat.

JOCK: Oh no DB. Don't tell me the government's going to give back all the treasure we've looted from around the world, with scant regard for the culture of anyone but ourselves and complete lack of reverence for centuries old religious beliefs?

DICK BARTON: Certainly not.

JOCK: Och thank heavens for that. What then?

DICK BARTON: Now that the light of dawn has touched one of the three stones of Ahkan Rah a terrible curse has been released on the three archaeologists who disturbed that Pharaoh's tomb. Piggy must be warned, we're in great danger.

JOCK: We?

DICK BARTON: Yes, Jock old chap. I don't suppose you've ever thought of me in khaki shorts have you?

JOCK: No, but I do think a side parting would give you a look of Lesley Howard.

DICK BARTON: Ah those were heady days. The first field trip of the Cambridge Light Operatic Archaeological society. There was Hugo 'Swanker' White, Julian 'Piggy' Petherington and me.

JOCK: Did you have an amusing public school nickname, DB?

DICK BARTON: Quiet Jock, I'm telling a story.
(*He joins in a flashback showing him and his school friends, PIGGY and SWANKER, as young archeologists.*)

Three Little Archaeologists

DICK BARTON: (*Sings.*)

THREE LITTLE ARCHAEOLOGISTS
YOUNG AND DASHING OPTIMISTS
FACING TROUBLE WITH OUR FISTS
ADVENTURE WAS OUR GAME.

PIGGY: (*Sings.*)

BOOTY WAS IN ALL OUR THOUGHTS

SWANKER: (*Sings.*)

WE WERE MODERN ARGONAUTS

DICK BARTON: (*Sings.*)

LOOKING SPLENDID IN OUR SHORTS

ALL: (*Sing.*)

WHAT AN INSPIRING THREE
DAYS WERE LONG AND NIGHTS WERE SCARY
TRUDGING THE SAHARA PRAIRIE

PIGGY: (*Sings.*)

PRICK'LY HEAT AND DYSENTRY

SWANKER: (*Sings.*)

SPREAD THROUGHOUT THE CHUMS.

ALL: (*Sing.*)

AND WE MISSED OUR MUMS.

DIGGING THROUGH THE SAND IS FOUL

YOU GET BLISTERS FROM YOUR TROWEL.

WE THOUGHT WE'D THROW IN THE TOWEL

DICK BARTON: (*Sings.*)

THEN AT LAST SUCCESS

THERE WAS HIDDEN 'NEATH THE SAND

OF THIS BRUTAL ANCIENT LAND

RICHES JUST AS WE HAD PLANNED

IN A PHARAOH'S TOMB.

WE WERE FEELING SO TERRIF

(*Slowing right down.*)

PIGGY: (*Sings.*)

THEN I READ THE HIEROGLYPH

SWANKER: (*Sings.*)

THE PRICE WE'D PAY COULD BE HORRIF-IC,

ALL: (*Sing.*)

MUMMYS, GHOSTS AND WORSE.

FROM AN ANCIENT CURSE.

DICK BARTON: For three days and nights Piggy studied the ancient hieroglyphic without sleeping. He discovered that the ancient guardians of the tomb did not consider it had been violated unless it's contents were touched by the light of dawn. So we resealed the tomb leaving its treasures to the darkness. But temptation had grown too much for Swanker. He had taken the sapphire Marta wore tonight, promising to keep it safely from the risen sun.

JOCK: Until this morning.

DICK BARTON: Quite right, when the curse was reactivated. So we must find Piggy to see if his subsequent studies can provide us with any protection. If only I knew what became of Swanker. He could be in great danger.

JOCK: Why was he called Swanker?

DICK BARTON: Ah, with his fine clothes and impeccable manners he was the swankiest boy in the third year dorm. His bed was next to mine and sometimes I'd watch him swanking all night.

JOCK: How wonderful! And 'Piggy'.

DICK BARTON: The young rascal could pig his way through a tuckbox like it was going out of fashion. Ah! The golden memories of public school life. I can't think it's the same in a secondary modern.

JOCK: No indeed. And you DB? What was your nick name?

DICK BARTON: Ah! Here we are 'The British Museum'.

BBC ANNOUNCER: And so the courageous crimefighters carry the gorgeous body of Marta Heartburn to the chambers of Piggy Petherington, deep in the bowels of the British Museum. It is here that Piggy has made many years study of Ancient Egyptian burial rights. As they await his arrival, our friends stare in awed silence at the grisly souvenirs of the long dead.

(*DICK BARTON, JOCK and MARTA are in a chamber crammed with mummy cases and scary masks. MARTA is lying covered with a cloth on some kind of slab.*)

JOCK: Och, go on tell us what your nickname was.

DICK BARTON: Jock do you understand the term awed silence?

JOCK: What was it though? Shall I try and guess?

DICK BARTON: The Barton name needs no embellishments. It stands sure and proud, like a rock against the tide of foul play and twisted dealings. The other chaps sensed that. There was no nick name.

(*PIGGY arrives.*)

PIGGY: Well I never, it's Barbara Barton. How are you Babs?

DICK BARTON: It's Dick Barton these days, old man. Tea-time radio star.

PIGGY: Oh I know, I always tune in. How does it go? (*He hums* Holiday For Strings.)

DICK BARTON: I think you'll find it's – (*Correctly, hums* The Devil's Gallop.)

PIGGY: Oh yes. D'you know it makes me laugh sometimes. Who'd have guessed, I tell the sarcophagi, who'd have guessed that's the same Babs Barton who used to steal into matron's room and try on her –

DICK BARTON: Yes, well I think there comes a time to put such childish matters behind us. Piggy, I have to tell you we're in grave danger.

PIGGY: How so, Babs?

JOCK: (*Innocently joining in.*) Och yes, do tell Barbara.

DICK BARTON: Piggy, could I have a little word (*He pulls him out of earshot of JOCK.*) The old nickname thing. I don't think it's a good idea any more, not in front of the lower ranks. Bad for morale, that sort of thing.

PIGGY: Understood.

DICK BARTON: (*Out loud again.*) I'm afraid it's the curse of Ahkan Rah!

PIGGY: But it can't be. We never brought our plunder up into the light.

DICK BARTON: You're forgetting the sapphire that Swanker pocketed. It fell into the wrong hands Piggy old chap. This woman stole it. She was wearing it around her neck when the sun rose this morning.

(*He removes the cloth covering MARTA's face.*)

JOCK: (*Helpfully.*) She's dead.

DICK BARTON: Yes, thank you Jock.

JOCK: Sorry.

PIGGY: But this is extraordinary. This woman had the sapphire you say?

DICK BARTON: Quite so. It seems that Swanker fell for her charms.

PIGGY: But she is…she is…this is extraordinary. (*Lifts his arms in prayer.*) Oh guardians of the ancients, all praise to you that have restored your fairest daughter to her destiny down through the mists of countless centuries.

DICK BARTON: Piggy have you been getting enough fresh air lately? Early rising, an ice-cold shower and an hour in the gymnasium will have you back to sorts in no time.

PIGGY: You don't understand. Do you not recognise this woman's face from years ago?

DICK BARTON: I don't think so...I...

PIGGY: Think man, think. Think back to the tomb of Ahkan Rah. What do you remember?

DICK BARTON: (*Reverently.*) We had egg sandwiches.

PIGGY: Not that. There in the hieroglyph this face stared out at us. The figure of an ancient queen. Here is a copy I made. A crude record – but you see my point. (*He holds up a really poor stick person drawing.*)

DICK BARTON: Good God. The resemblance is uncanny. But it cannot be the same face. This (*MARTA.*) is the face of a foreign spy and this (*The drawing.*) is the face of...

PIGGY: Queen Nefatartie. Beloved consort of Pharaoh Ahkan Rah and the original owner of the sapphire. Perhaps the jewel has come home. Do you have the sapphire?

JOCK: It's right here, sir.

PIGGY: Pop it down in the corner, I'll examine it later. NOT ON THAT! That table is a highly prized artefact. Over there by that pile of old rocks.

JOCK: Where it says 'Elgin Marbles'?

PIGGY: (*Ignoring JOCK.*) All this means that we are in mortal danger. There can be no doubt that the mummy who guards the tomb will come looking for us.

DICK BARTON: A stinking corpse, lumbering from beyond the grave, its rotting, rancid flesh held in place by bandages.

JOCK: Crepe?

DICK BARTON: I'm afraid it's true Jock old chap.

JOCK: No I mean are they crepe bandages?

DICK BARTON: Jock would you go and wait in the Bentley. Read your Eagle comic or something.

JOCK: Yes DB. (*He leaves.*)

PIGGY: I'm very worried, I don't mind telling you Barbara.

DICK BARTON: Don't fret old chap. We'll get to the bottom of this. Go over all the papyrus again, see if you can't find some clue as to how we can protect ourselves from the mummy. I'll go back to HQ and see if I can't track down Swanker, he must be warned about the mummy and he may have some information that could help us. Let's meet up at 0900 hours. Synchronise watches.

(*They both look at their watches. DICK BARTON taps his. It has obviously stopped.*)

Never mind. I'll meet you on the hour between Workers' Playtime and Housewife's Choice.

BBC ANNOUNCER: And so the Barton Bentley speeds towards HQ. So many thoughts are tumbling around that noble head. Half-remembered prophecies in foreign lands, snatched conversations on the banks of the Nile, three young archaeologists, an ancient king, a beautiful queen, a tragic death, and a deadly curse. Back at the Barton HQ the secret agent offers to de-brief his Scots assistant.

JOCK: We don't wear them under our kilt sir.

DICK BARTON: No Jock, 'de-brief'. You don't understand. I'm going to tell you the legend of the Pharaoh's tomb. (*Sings.*)

The Legend Of Ahkan Rah

IN A STRANGE DISTANT LAND
WHERE THE PYRAMIDS ARE
THERE ONCE RULED A MIGHTY KING OF EGYPT
THE PHARAOH AHKAN RAH.

HE HAD POWER INDEED
ALL WOULD COWER AT HIS NAME
HE HAD WEALTH BEYOND IMAGINATION
HE'D PUT CROESUS TO SHAME

JOCK: (*Sings.*)

WHO'D PLAY HIM IN A FILM?
WOULD IT BE LESLIE HOWARD?
BASIL RATHBONE CAN BE QUITE COMMANDING

DICK BARTON: (*Sings.*)

NO I THINK DEAR NOËL COWARD.

(*We see Pharoah AHKAN RAH. He sings Coward-like.*)

Single Pharaoh Seeks A Girlfriend

AIIKAN RAH: (*Sings.*)

SINGLE PHARAOH SEEKS A GIRLFRIEND
SOMEONE NOT AVERSE TO ROYAL FUNCTIONS
I GET VERY LONELY.
BEING HEAVEN'S ONLY
LIVING INCARNATION'S
NOT WITHOUT ITS OBLIGATIONS.
APPLICATIONS TO THE PALACE
ALL ENQUIRES ANSWERED WITH A PORTRAIT
LOOKS ARE QUITE IMPORTANT
SHE SHOULD HAVE DEPORTMENT
AGILE AS A PUMA
SHE SHOULD HAVE A SENSE OF HUMOUR
BEING QUEEN'S TOO COMPLICATED
FOR THE TYPE OF GIRL I'VE DATED
THERE MUST BE ONE LOTUS FLOWER
WHO CAN HANDLE TOTAL POWER
OTHER PHARAOHS TRIED INBREEDING
BUT I CAN'T SEE THAT SUCCEEDING
HAVE YOU SEEN MY UGLY SISTER?
ONLY RATTLESNAKES HAVE KISSED HER
SINGLE PHARAOH SEEKS A GIRLFRIEND
PREFERABLY NOT A BLOOD RELATION
COUSIN CLEOPATRA'S
A SYCOPHANTIC FLATTERER
LITTLE AUNT AIDA
HAS DISTINCTLY GONE TO SEED. A —
PHARAOH NEVER GETS TO MINGLE
OR CHAT TO PRETTY GIRLS AT DINNER PARTIES
IF YOU'RE A LITTLE SWEETIE
BE MY NEFERTITI
CROCODILE MY NUMBER NOW

(*The VIZIER approaches AHKAN RAH.*)

VIZIER: Oh mighty one. The costume you've ordered
has arrived.

AHKAN RAH: Splendid, splendid. I will disguise myself and move amongst my people to find a queen worthy to rule with me. The moon rests on the seventh mantle of the seventh house of Rah, let the night's dark revels commence on the swift fleeting wings of Hathor's cup-bearer. (*Beat.*) D'you know any good bars where one can pick up girls?

DICK BARTON: And so the mighty pharaoh Ahkan Rah stole out of the palace under the watchful eye of the god Horus and a thousand, thousand twinkling stars. For many hours he wandered amongst his ancient and noble people. The aromas of the spice market and the colours of the bazaar seemed to his unaccustomed senses more glorious then the rich perfumes of Arabia or the precious jewels in his treasury. Where, the mighty king pondered, could he find a woman whose beauty eclipsed the wonders of his ancient kingdom?

(*The stage becomes that of a seedy strip joint in ancient Egypt. The MC addresses the audience.*)

MC: Good evening ladies and gentlemen and welcome to Cairo's premiere cabaret venue The Needle's Eye – even the camels are passing through! Alright settle down, settle down – the stripper will be on in a minute. First of all I want to welcome a few new faces in our audience this evening. A big welcome to the Karnack Rotary Club, the lads have got a 'sharra' all the way up the Nile delta to be with us here this evening. Let's give them a nice Needle's Eye welcome (*He gets the audience to applaud.*) Who else have we got in tonight? I do believe it's the Aswan Golden Years Club. Lovely to have the old folks back with us again. And now, without further ado, the moment you've all been waiting for. She put the smile on the Sphinx and the 'ai ai ai!' in Cairo. A big Needle's Eye welcome for Miss Nefatartie!

(*NEFATARTIE appears on stage. She looks like Salomé and sounds like a rusty hinge with a squeaky Brooklyn showgirl accent.*)

Talent

NEFATARTIE: (*Sings.*)

WHEN I WAS YOUNG
I HAD A DREAM
TO STAR UPON THE STAGE
I'D TREAD THE BOARDS
AND CHARM THE HOARDS
WHO'D MAKE ME ALL THE RAGE
BUT FROM TAIWAN TO AZERBAIJAN
EACH SHOW I'D DO WOULD CLOSE
CAUSE THE ONLY TALENT I POSSESS
IS TAKING OFF MY CLOTHES
I STARTED OUT IN BABYLON
WITH A DANCE OF SEVEN VEILS
THEN I PROGRESSED WITH SOME SUCCESS
TO A DANCE OF SEVEN SNAILS
WHEN THAT GREW TIRED
I WAS INSPIRED TO DANCE WITH SEVEN NAILS
BUT WHO NEEDS SEVEN ANYTHING
WHEN YOU'RE ENTERTAINING MALES

SO I CAN'T ACT AND I CAN'T DANCE
MY VOICE COULD KILL A BULL
THIS ROUTINE'S DUMB
BUT THEY STILL COME
TILL EVERY SEAT IS FULL
AND SO THE SECRET OF SUCCESS
IS SKIP THAT ACTING CLASS
CAUSE WHO NEEDS TALENT ANYWAY
FOR WAGGLING YOUR –

(*AHKAN RAH interrupts her.*)

The Proposal

AHKAN RAH: (*Sings.*)

DON'T SAY ANOTHER WORD YOU STAR
YOU'LL BE THE QUEEN OF PHARAOH AHKAN RAH
COME TAKE MY HAND

WE'LL RULE THE LAND

YOU CAN RETIRE THAT TASSELLED BRA.

(As the music resolves.)

DICK BARTON: And so the land of Egypt began 40 days of feasting and celebration of the royal match. Time passed and seven harvest moons waxed and waned over the majestic waters of the Nile and the contented pharaoh and his queen. But a snake lay coiled at the heart of this happy union. Not for the wretched pharaoh the joyous fruitful state of matrimony enjoyed by our own dear royal family. Although he lavished every luxury on the girl, hers was a restless spirit and her affections shifted as the desert sand. Word reached the divine ruler that his queen had taken a lover.

(AHKAN RAH consults the VIZIER.)

AHKAN RAH: Who is it? I'll tear him limb from limb, I'll have him disembowelled and fed to the crocodiles.

VIZIER: Your spies tell us that public disembowelment would not be wise. The queen's lover is a rebel leader who enjoys great popularity with the Hamadi people. Were you seen to cause him harm it could spark great civil unrest.

AHKAN RAH: This is intolerable. What is the name of this fiend in human form?

VIZIER: The local women call him the Colossus of Cartouche.

AHKAN RAH: I know the fellow. Hairy, outdoor sort of chap. I don't know what all that 'Colossus' business is about. Why do the girls call him that? He's not much taller than me? *(Beat.)* What does she see in him anyway? What's he got that I haven't?

Thinking Big

NEFATARTIE: *(Sings.)*

I'VE HAD SMALL, SMALL WAS FINE

IT WAS FUN, I'D BEGUN, IT WAS MINE.

THAT WAS SMALL

IT WOULD PALL
NOW I'M BORED, I WANT BIG
WANT IT ALL.
TWINKLE ON LITTLE STARS
I WANT MORE
I WANT VENUS AND MARS.
ALL THE MICE LOOK THE SAME
MICE ARE NICE BUT I WANT BIGGER GAME.

DICK BARTON: As months passed the lonely pharaoh became inconsolable, wandering the corridors of the royal palace as a dead man. Their tragic operetta played out against the backdrop of mighty Egypt.

AHKAN RAH: (*Sings.*)

ONE HUNDRED NIGHTS I'VE SLEPT ALONE
THE LOVE SHE FELT FOR ME HAS FLOWN
MY HEART'S IN TWO
WHAT CAN I DO,
TO WIN HER BACK TO STAY?
I CANNOT SLEEP, I CAN NOT EAT
I'M FADING FAST AND FACE DEFEAT
THE MORE I TRY
WITH GIFTS I BUY
THE MORE SHE TURNS AWAY

DICK BARTON: The pharoah even presented his love with a magnificent ruby the size of a tennis ball; many men had killed for its legendary beauty but still the queen rejected him and made a gift of the blood-red jewel to her lover.

NEFATARTIE: (*Sings.*)

HE THINKS BIG, BIG IS BEST
BIG IS GRAND, BIG IS GREAT, BEATS THE REST
HE HAS DREAMS
THERE'S A PLAN.
HE'S A HUNK OF A CHUNK OF A MAN.
LITTLE GUYS COME AND GO.
HONEY, WHEN MY GUY'S COMING, YOU KNOW
LITTLE BOYS CRY AND SULK.
THAT'S WHY I LIKE TO ORDER IN BULK.

(The VIZIER approaches NEFATARTIE.)

VIZIER: Your majesty. I bring grave news. Your husband, the pharaoh, is dead. He died of a broken heart.

NEFATARTIE: Well, did he leave any instructions about how to run the empire. I mean, how do you work this thing?

VIZIER: Your majesty need not trouble herself with the day to day running of the state.

NEFATARTIE: *(Relieved.)* Okay but I still get to wave to the crowd from the balcony, right?

VIZIER: I don't think Your Majesty quite understands. When a pharaoh dies there are certain burial rights which have to be adhered to: the queen is buried alive with the pharoah.

DICK BARTON: Entombed for ever beneath the sand. The faithful vizier threw himself on his sword as was the custom. He was mummified and buried alongside his master so that he might protect the tomb from those in centuries to come who would desecrate it and steal the contents. It is this half-man, half-monster that we must fear tonight. The Colossus was inconsolable and retired with all the jewels the queen had bought him to a cave in the mountains. He lived out his days in anonymous exile until he too died of a broken heart in sorrow at what he had done. So there you are Jock, now you know the whole tragic story behind the tomb of Ahkan Rah.

JOCK: And not a moment too soon. I'm really going to have to run for it if I'm going to make my latest evening class.

DICK BARTON: Ah good chap. Wonderful to hear you persevered. Did they let you on the woodwork course this time?

JOCK: No I'm studying 'Representations of women in post-war European literature'. Do you think there may be a ground-breaking, pre-feminist role model in this adventure DB?

DICK BARTON: Good heavens, no. This one's far too dangerous for girls.

JOCK: Righty-ho! Now are you sure you'll be okay if I leave you here on your own? Snowy should be back in a minute.

DICK BARTON: I'll be perfectly alright. Why shouldn't I be?

JOCK: Well, I thought you might be feeling a bit nervous what with the mummy after you?

DICK BARTON: Certainly not. We Bartons have nerves of steel. It'll take more than some foreign hocus pocus, jiggery-pokery to frighten me whilst I've my trusty Remington at my side.

(*The lights go out.*)

DICK BARTON: What was that?

JOCK: Och. I must have forgotten to feed the meter. There's a torch in here somewhere.

(*He shines the torch straight into the bandaged face of a MUMMY. DICK BARTON and JOCK scream. But in fact it's SNOWY with his face bandaged up.*)

SNOWY: Alright me old muckers.

DICK BARTON/JOCK: Snowy!

SNOWY: How you diddling? The doc says I've got to keep these bandages on the old boat race until the rash goes away. I bet I look a real state and no mistake. I gave Mrs Horrocks a real shock on the apples and pairs. I'll go and put a shilling in the metre.

(*He exits. JOCK now shines the light at DICK BARTON's face.*)

JOCK: Are you alright boss? You look like you've had a nasty shock.

DICK BARTON: (*In shock.*) I'll be alright. Just pour me a very large scotch, press a damp flannel to my head and call for Matron.

BBC ANNOUNCER: Was ever greater peril faced by a tea- time wireless celebrity? And as if that that weren't rootin'- tootin'-slap-me-round-the-chops-with a-wet-kipper thrilling enough another danger lies in wait for Dick Barton. Piggy Petherington's interest in the long dead Nefatartie is more than academic. The extraordinary resemblance between that ancient queen and the evil temptress Marta Heartburn has awoken unwholesome desires in the Egyptologist. Listeners of a nervous disposition may wish to go and put the cat out as we eavesdrop on the wretched man's invocation of a pagan god.

(*PIGGY stands over MARTA's body –still lying on a slab.*)

Piggy's Prayer

PIGGY: (*Sings.*)

AMON RAH

FATHER OF THE PHARAOHS

HIGHEST ANCIENT DEITY

SEND YOUR POWER

TO YOUR HUMBLE SERVANT

BRING MY QUEEN TO LIFE FOR ME

I'VE WORSHIPPED HER FROM HISTORY

AND NOW THE GODS BRING HER TO ME

DORMANT IN THE BODY OF THIS GIRL

TONIGHT MY LOVE YOU'LL LIVE AGAIN

TOGETHER WE'LL BEGIN OUR REIGN

THE SCROLL OF DESTINY CAN NOW UNFURL.

BARTON ALWAYS WAS A FOOL

I HATED HIM AT PUBLIC SCHOOL

FROM NOW ON I'M THE TEACHER AND HE'LL LEARN

I'LL HAVE HIM GROVEL AT MY FEET

REVENGE WILL FEEL SO VERY SWEET

THE WORM HE BULLIED'S REALLY GOING TO TURN.

(*Music continues. Lots of choral 'ah's.*)

(*Spoken.*) Great spirit of the long dead queen rise up from the swirling waters of the Nile, from the shifting sands of the Sahara, from the blood-red scar of the Egyptian sunset, from the enigmatic smile of the secret Sphinx and live again in the beautiful body of this woman.

(*Thunderclap. MARTA, now NEFATARTIE, sits up on the slab.*)

It works, she breathes again. Speak to me my angel of the night, speak to me from the bosom of this mortal woman, let your voice echo across the threshold of the underworld to your new destiny, as the consort of my brooding malevolent evil.

(*MARTA now has the vulgar squeaky 'Noo Yawk' accent of NEFATARTIE.*)

NEFATARTIE: Hey, get a gal a drink can't you. My mouth's as dry as a camel's armpit.

PIGGY: (*Triumphantly sings.*)

COME MY QUEEN

TAKE YOUR PLACE BESIDE ME

TOGETHER WE WILL CONQUER ALL

WE'LL BE WICKED, CRUEL AND RUTHLESS

TIME TO EVEN UP THE SCORE

(*Another clap of thunder. He laughs maniacally.*)

BBC ANNOUNCER: (*Covering his eyes and now peeping out.*) It's alright, you can come out from behind the sofa now. So whilst Dick Barton ponders his next move back at HQ and Piggy Petherington turns to EFIL, what has become of the third member of that once merry band? Where, I hear you ask, where oh where is Swanker? Wonder no more as the magic of the airwaves and the latest developments in wireless technology whisk us thousands of miles away to the British Forces Club in Cairo.

(*We see the silhouettes of British army OFFICERS in their club. The silhouettes are drinking brandy, talking, smoking. We hear tinkling cocktail music. SWANKER staggers onto the stage. He is dressed like Laurence of Arabia in the famous scene in which he arrives from the desert at the British Club. Laurence of Arabia type underscoring.*)

SWANKER: Water, water if I could just have a glass of water.

BRIT: Good God. Natives aren't allowed in here.

BRIT: Gungadin, throw this filthy blighter out into the street.

SWANKER: Please, I have to get to a telephone. I have to make a vital phone call to London.

BRIT: Just a minute. That's no native.

BRIT: Who the devil are you, sir?

SWANKER: I have lived so long with the desert people that my western name has been lost to me.

BRIT: Good, God! I know you. It's Hugo White isn't?

BRIT: Not old Swanker White?

SWANKER: Please, I have vital information for you about the military stability of the desert tribes across Egypt and the Arabian countries but I must make a phone call to London.

BRIT: But this is extraordinary.

BRIT: (*Proposing a toast.*) Gentlemen, I give you Swanker of Arabia.

BRITS: Hoorah!

SWANKER: The telephone please! And a glass of water.

BRIT: This way, old boy.

(*SWANKER passes through. As he passes:*)

BRIT: Tell us, when the desert chappies go on holiday do they make sand castles as we do?

SWANKER: (*On the telephone.*) Hello, operator...I need to get through to London. I have an urgent call for Barbara Barton...Sorry, Dick Barton – special agent...No madame I'm afraid I can't get you his autograph I'm in Cairo...Yes I believe he is as tall as he sounds on the wireless. Yes I'll hold the line. (*Soft and longing.*) Operator? How is dear old Blighty? Operator? Are there still cucumber sandwiches for tea? And does the sound of ball against willow still cut through the warm summer afternoons on the village green? Does the sunlight still shimmer across the manicured lawns as beautiful girls in white walk arm in arm with handsome youths in crisp linen?...What do you mean you live in Peckham? (*Gives up.*) Just put me through to Dick Barton.

(*Lights down on him and up on the BBC ANNOUNCER.*)

BBC ANNOUNCER: Wires hum, spark and whirr across the continents as Swanker's call comes through to Barton HQ in London. But our hero is in no position to answer, held captive as he is, by his one-time school chum Piggy

Petherington. All the frustrations of those salad days now spew forth in a tide of recriminations.

(*As he speaks DICK BARTON and SNOWY are revealed tied back-to-back with their trouser legs rolled up, standing in a bowl of water. There is a second bowl of water standing close by with a skull and cross bones emblazoned on the side. PIGGY presides over them with a gun. A telephone is ringing.*)

PIGGY: And another thing, there was that time when I wanted to be Juliet in the school play and you said I was so fat we'd have to reinforce the balcony but everyone knew it was because you wanted to play it and you'd already picked out the frock.

DICK BARTON: (*Calmly and politely.*) I say Pigs, if we're going to be much longer do you think you could answer the telephone?

(*It stops.*)

Oh dear, I do hope it wasn't a matter of national importance regarding the safety of the free world.

JOCK: Or the dry cleaner to say your other mackintosh is ready.

PIGGY: You will have no need of gaberdine when I've finished with you.

JOCK: Aberdeen?

PIGGY/DICK BARTON: GABERDINE!

JOCK: Where's that then?

DICK BARTON: Steady there Jock.

JOCK: Sorry DB.

PIGGY: You will notice that you are standing in a bowl of water.

DICK BARTON: Ah yes.

PIGGY: You will also notice that adjacent to it is a second bowl of water.

DICK BARTON: And swimming in bowl B, would that be half-a-dozen of the world's most deadly piranha fish? Capable of stripping a herd of buffalo clean to the bone in 40 seconds flat?

PIGGY: Well spotted.

DICK BARTON: Thank you very much.

PIGGY: But not quite! This particular mutation gnaws through the bone as well. They've been cross-bred with electric eels to give their jaws the unstoppable momentum of a chainsaw. Now, you'll notice that suspended above bowl B is a wireless set connected to an intricate collection of pulleys. Which in turn is linked to a clock. At this time tomorrow night the clock will cause the wireless set to switch on at the start of the Billy Cotton Big Band Show.

DICK BARTON: Good old Billy.

PIGGY: Not quite again, I'm afraid. Billy and his toe-tapping troop of tunesters have been captured by the forces of EFIL and replaced by dangerous international anarchist muscicians.

DICK BARTON: Good God!

PIGGY: As the programme begins, the counterfeit Billy will lead the EFIL dance band in the popular air 'Scots Wahay' which we happen to know is a favourite of your homely housekeeper Mrs Horrocks.

JOCK: Indeed it is, you devil.

PIGGY: The variation on the theme of the much loved Scottish folk song will sound across the airways and ring throughout your headquarters here. Its jaunty tune will cause your housekeeper Mrs Horrocks to tap her foot in time to the music in her attic room above us. These vibrations will activate a series of pulleys lowering the suspended wireless set into the bowl of piranhas beneath it.

DICK BARTON: Great heavens that will drive them crazy.

PIGGY: Quite so. As you have correctly observed the piranha aversion to popular dance music is well documented. They will leap from bowl B across to the water beneath you and there they will feast until Mr Dick 'big-shot-head-boy-rugger-cricket-and-home-economics-champion-three years running' Barton will just be a lowly link in the food chain.

DICK BARTON: You won't get away with this! You always were a snivelling little creep. Swanker and I only let you be our friend because your ma sent you brandy fruitcake back from the hols.

PIGGY: Your taunts can't hurt me now Barton. (*Suddenly all pathetic.*) That's not true about the cake is it? (*Confident again.*) Well, what care I when I have the love of the most beautiful woman in history? I must return to her side. I've wasted enough time on you. Enjoy the music, won't you? (*He laughs maniacally and sweeps out.*)

DICK BARTON: I wonder what he meant about the most beautiful woman in history.

JOCK: Don't worry about that DB we've only got 20 minutes to live.

DICK BARTON: Yes, it's a tough one alright. I'll have to think up something quite ingenious to get us out of this one.

BBC ANNOUNCER: What was Swanker's urgent news? Will Piggy Petherington find happiness with Queen Nefatartie? Is her bandaged bodyguard a mummified match for Barton? Or does the super-sleuth face a dastardly death at the hand of the BBC Big Band? To find out tune in after the interval for the next exciting instalment of Dick Barton – Special Agent. (*Dick Barton theme.*)

End of Act One.

ACT TWO

The Dick Barton theme takes us to the BBC ANNOUNCER.

BBC ANNOUNCER: Welcome back. At Buckingham Palace itself Piggy Petherington prepares to introduce his new gal to the cream of London society.
(We move to Buckingham Palace. PIGGY is looking anxiously around him, forking in mouthfuls of a little cake from a plate. Beside him NEFATARTIE looks bored. The MUMMY stands between them staring at PIGGY. A pianist plays a turgid tune.)

PIGGY: Why does he keep staring at me like that?

NEFATARTIE: *(To the MUMMY.)* Relax, Tuten. How many times do I have to tell you? The tubby Brit is our meal ticket.

PIGGY: He nearly frightened me to death this morning looming out of the airing cupboard like that.

NEFATARTIE: You startled him.

PIGGY: Well I don't see why you had to bring him to Buckingham Palace with us.

NEFATARTIE: He wants to see the sights.

PIGGY: Now darling when the King speaks to you remember what I taught you.

NEFATARTIE: Yeh, sure. Don't keep going over it already, 'How do you do. How do you do.' The rain in Spain rains mainly on the friggin' plain. He's a guy isn't he? Honey I've had plenty of kings on their knees before me and they wasn't begging for mercy neither.

PIGGY: Now darling, that's just the kind of thing…

NEFATARTIE: Let's go make out.

PIGGY: Cupcake you are insatiable. We were 'making out' all night. I've 'made out' more in the 48 hours since I've known you than the whole of the rest of my life. I'm exhausted.

NEFATARTIE: Yeh and finally you're just about getting the basics.

A FOOTMAN: His majesty the King.
(*KING GEORGE enters.*)

PIGGY: Your Majesty.

KING GEORGE: Good heavens, it's young Piggy
Petherington isn't it? Weren't you at school with that
rascal nephew of mine Hugo.

PIGGY: That's right Your Majesty.

KING GEORGE: And if I'm not mistaken young Dicky
Barton. The three of you were inseparable.

NEFATARTIE: I think I'm gunna puke.

PIGGY: Your Majesty may I introduce my gal?

KING GEORGE: What a pleasure to meet you.

NEFATARTIE: Whatever.

KING GEORGE: I hope you young people aren't finding
my little party too dull.

NEFATARTIE: Can I be frank Your Maj.

KING GEORGE: Please do.

PIGGY: Please don't.

NEFATARTIE: Your party sucks. They got more laughs in
the ancient Book of the Dead. Know what I'm saying?

KING GEORGE: My goodness.

NEFATARTIE: Yeh, you wanna liven things up around
here. (*To the pianist.*) Hey honey, you gunna pep the
music up or do I have to come over there and stick
a lighted cigar up your butt.

PIGGY: This is a disaster.

The Pharaoh Rag

NEFATARTIE: (*Sings.*)

THERE'S A LITTLE DANCE
WE DO WHERE I COME FROM
IT'S CALLED 'THE PHARAOH RAG'
IF YOU STUFFY BRITS CAN LEARN IT TOO
YOUR PARTIES SOON'LL NEVER DRAG
(*She demonstrates.*)
SHIMMY DOWN, STEP OUT TO THE RIGHT
SLIDE YOUR LEFT FOOT OVER
BRING YOUR KNEES IN TIGHT

MAKE OUT LIKE A CHICKEN

THEN REPEAT

SOON YOU'LL HAVE A PARTY BUMPIN' TO THE BEAT

PIGGY: (*Sings.*)

PLEASE DARLING, THIS IS NOT

THE TIME OR PLACE

FOR SUCH VULGARITY

WON'T YOU PLEASE EXCUSE US EVERYONE

WE'LL LEAVE YOUR HOSPITALITY.

KING GEORGE: (*Sings.*)

NONSENSE JULIAN YOUR GAL'S A TREAT

IT'S HIGH TIME THAT WE FOUND OUR DANCING FEET.

I'VE NOT DANCED A STEP SINCE '42

WON'T YOU TELL US, MADAME, WHAT WE OUGHT TO DO?

NEFATARTIE: (*Spoken.*) You'll love it. (*Sings dancing.*)

NEXT FLICK YOUR FEET OUT FROM BEHIND

AS IF TO KICK THE SAND AWAY

ADD A BILLY-HOP TO EITHER SIDE

AND DO A HULA-HULA SWAY

KING GEORGE: (*Spoken.*) I think I understand.
(*KING GEORGE and NEFATARTIE dance.*)

KING GEORGE/NEFATARTIE: (*Sing.*)

SHIMMY DOWN AND STEP OUT TO THE RIGHT

SLIDE YOUR LEFT FOOT OVER

BRING YOUR KNEES IN TIGHT

MAKE OUT LIKE A CHICKEN

THEN REPEAT

SOON YOU'LL HAVE A PARTY BUMPIN' TO THE BEAT

KING GEORGE: (*Spoken.*) Come on everyone!
(*Everyone including the MUMMY and BBC ANNOUNCER
join in a swinging dance break for the length of the verse.
Lots of "I say isn't this fun" etc. etc. then everyone sings.*)

ALL: (*Sing.*)

SHIMMY DOWN AND STEP OUT TO THE RIGHT

SLIDE YOUR LEFT FOOT OVER

BRING YOUR KNEES IN TIGHT

MAKE OUT LIKE A CHICKEN

DON'T YOU FLAG

RIDE THAT RHYTHM WHEN YOUR FEELINGS START TO SAG

(*Big finish.*)

NOW THE JOINT IS JUMPIN'

BOY WE'RE REALLY BUMPIN'

CAUSE WE'RE DOING THE PHARAOH RAG.

KING GEORGE: Goodness me. I haven't had so much fun since Von Ribbontroff fleeced me at strip poker.

(*A telegram is handed to KING GEORGE.*)

KING GEORGE: My word! Here's a bit of good news for you Piggy old chap, it's from nephew Hugo.

NEFATARTIE: Swanker!

KING GEORGE: No really it is. It seems the young pup is flying home. He wants to raise the money for a new expedition. He says he's found a map showing the tomb of some ancient Egyptian rebel leader rumoured to have been buried with a legendary ruby.

(*NEFATARTIE faints.*)

Good heavens. Poor gal. It must have been all that hula-hula-ing.

PIGGY: She'll be alright in a moment sir. She just needs a little rest.

KING GEORGE: Highly-strung little filly, eh? That's how I used to like 'em. Well come on everyone. Who's for musical bumps in the ballroom? Von Ribbontroff rules.

(*The MUMMY, PIGGY and NEFATARTIE are left alone. She recovers very quickly.*)

NEFATARTIE: Did you hear that? Did you? Your puny little friend has found the final resting place of my darling one.

PIGGY: I don't understand.

NEFATARTIE: The Colossus of Cartouche. My best guy. Ours was the most passionate love affair of all time. When we'd make out the skies would rumble and the mountains would shake.

PIGGY: Was he…was he…was he better at 'making out' then me?

NEFATARTIE: Honey, let me tell you.

PIGGY: (*Sulky.*) I see, well, naturally you'll want to visit and pop a bunch of roses at the old graveside.

NEFATARTIE: You bagel brain! Don't you understand? The ruby was a gift the pharaoh gave me and I gave to my Colossus. If Swanker's found the tomb it's still going to be there.

PIGGY: Good for Swanker.

NEFATARTIE: He isn't going to get within a flea's tit of that stone. It's mine you understand – mine! And when he arrives in England we're going to kill him just as finally as we bumped off Dick Barton.

PIGGY: The old wireless in the bucket of piranhas trick?

NEFATARTIE: Not this time. Come my pet. (*The MUMMY lumbers forward.*) I think it's time for Tuten to have his fun. (*To the MUMMY.*) Go kill the archaeologist, there's a good boy. Go kill.

(*The MUMMY lumbers off.*)

MUMMY: Kill.

PIGGY: How wizard! Then we'll steal the map, return to Egypt, bag the treasure, be rich beyond our wildest dreams and we could open a little tea shop in Bournemouth.

(*He leaves in a daydream.*)

NEFATARTIE: Oh Colossus, in this world of pygmies, will I ever meet your like again?

Reprise – Thinking Big

WHO IS BIG ANYMORE?

WHO'S A RED-BLOODED, BUTCH CARNIVORE

WITH A DREAM

WITH SOME SCHEME

NOT SOME STIFF-UPPER-LIPPED BRITISH BORE.

ARE THERE GUYS STILL AROUND

WHO CAN WRESTLE A BEAR TO THE GROUND?

ONE WHO'LL CUSS, ONE WHO'LL FIGHT

AND BE ROUGH, TOUGH AND TENDER ALL NIGHT.

BBC ANNOUNCER: And so with British virility called into question, time is running out for Dick Barton and his loyal sidekick Jock. The hour fast approaches when Piggy Petherington's fiendish device will spring into deadly motion.

(*DICK BARTON and JOCK as we left them tied back-to-back, feet in water with the other bucket close by.*)

JOCK: You have to think of something quick DB, it's only minutes until Billy Cotton and the BBC Big Band are on the air. If only Snowy wasn't in the White City home for convalescing cockneys he could rescue us.

DICK BARTON: It looks like we're done for this time, old chap. Once the fake Billy lifts the baton on 'Scots Wahay' and the wireless descends nearer the water, those bone-crunching piranhas will be gnawing through feet in no time.

JOCK: Granny McNair always said that if I ate many more fish suppers I'd turn into one. I never thought she meant I'd be on the menu.

DICK BARTON: Just a minute. What did you say?

JOCK: Granny McNair always said –

DICK BARTON: 'Fish suppers' eh. What if we could… No, no it's a ridiculous idea.

JOCK: Go on DB.

DICK BARTON: It couldn't possibly work.

JOCK: It's got to be worth a try, we're running out of time.

DICK BARTON: What if we could persuade the piranhas that they're better off staying where they are.

JOCK: How could we do that?

DICK BARTON: By simulating an atmosphere so terrifying to fish that even the sound of the Billy Cotton Big Band won't drive them into the open. Quickly, in a loud clear voice reel off a list of Scottish fish delicacies.

JOCK: Uh – umm…

DICK BARTON: Come on, Jock!

(*We hear the wireless above crackle into life.*)

VOICE: (*From the wireless.*) Wakey! Wakey! Hello everyone out there in radio-land, it's the Billy Cotton Big Band here again and we're kicking off tonight's programme with a wee highland fling.

JOCK: (*Panicky.*) Boss!

The Fish Song

DICK BARTON: (*Sings, tentatively at first.*)

SCOTTISH SMOKED SALMON
WITH DILL AND ASPARAGUS
HALIBUT POACHED WITH
A SPRIG OF FRESH LEMONGRASS
CRAWFISH IN CHOWDER
AND SCALLOPS AND CAVIAR
SEA BASS WITH FENNEL
AND SOLE PROVENÇAL

(*Growing in confidence.*)
JOHN DORY FILLETED
THEN FRIED IN OLIVE OIL
MULLET WITH TARRAGON
AND LOBSTER THERMIDOR
BREAM BAKED IN BUTTER
AND CATFISH IN GUMBALI
ROLLMOPS AND KEDGEREE
STAR GAZY PIE
– Jock!

JOCK: Um – Ahhh…
DICK BARTON: (*Sings.*)

FRIED CALAMARI
AND PASTA WITH VONGOLE
SHARK STEAKS AND CHOWDER
AND OCTOPUS FRICASSEE
TERRINE OF TENCH
TURBOT, TUNA AND TROUT
(*There's a thumping from above in time to the music.*)
EEL COOKED AS ELVER
AND…JOCK HELP ME OUT!

(*The wireless set begins to lower towards the bucket of piranhas beneath it.*)
WHITING WITH WHITEBAIT
AND HERRING WITH HAKE
OYSTERS IN ASPIC

AND RAW PICKLED SKATE

MEDALLIONS OF MULLET

IN PUFF PASTRY SLIPS

PERCH DONE WITH PARSLEY

Jock? –

(*The wireless is just above the water.*)

JOCK: (*Triumphantly.*) – Haddock and Chips!
(*No piranhas jump out. The wireless set disappears into the water. There are sparks and steam and the sound of hissing and bubbles.*)

BOTH: It worked – hooray!
(*The phone starts ringing. MRS HORROCKS, the housekeeper, enters.*)

DICK BARTON: Mrs Horrocks! Has ever a fellow been so glad to see his housekeeper?

MRS HORROCKS: Oh I see you're playing your tying up games again Mr Barton, I don't know. Who's going to answer the telephone while you're having your shenanigans? That's the question. (*She answers the telephone.*) Hello. No, I'm sorry there's no one called Barbara here.

DICK BARTON: Um, Mrs Horrocks there's a slightest chance that might be for me.

MRS HORROCKS: No sir, he distinctly said Barbara.

DICK BARTON: Even so. I wonder, could you release us?
(*She unties DICK BARTON and JOCK.*)

MRS HORROCKS: I've said it before and I'll say it again. You've got some very funny friends. And I was in a very good mood as well. Enjoying a lovely broadcast by that nice Billy Cotton and his merry minstrels.

DICK BARTON: Mrs Horrocks. I'm afraid I've some very upsetting news for you. The Billy Cotton Big Band have been infiltrated by foreigners.

MRS HORROCKS: Great heavens, I shall never listen to their subversive broadcast again for fear of being brainwashed onto the slippery slopes of communism.

JOCK: I'll get over to Broadcasting House right away before the devils try Educating Archie. (*He rushes out.*)

MRS HORROCKS: Pray God no!

(*DICK BARTON picks up the phone.*)

DICK BARTON: Babs Barton here. I mean Dick Barton – Special Agent.

(*We can see SWANKER at the other end of the line.*)

SWANKER: Good to hear your voice after all this time. How are you, you young pup?

DICK BARTON: Matron?

SWANKER: No you chump. (*Sings a snatch of the old school song to the tune of* Boating Song.) 'Oh we're all boys together up in the third-year dorm with midnight feasts, and apple pie beds, and wizard pranks till dawn.'

DICK BARTON: Swanker!

SWANKER: Correctamento Babs.

DICK BARTON: Swanker! Where are you?

SWANKER: Here in Londinium old chap. Just flown in with the RAF from Cairo. I'm here to raise some money for a dig and to get the old gang back together. Listen, I think I've found a map for the burial chamber of the Colossus of Cartouche. Word is it contains the largest ruby in the world. We're going to be very, very rich.

DICK BARTON: You are very, very rich.

SWANKER: Yes, but I'm not letting that spoil the fun.

DICK BARTON: Listen old boy, you're in great danger. No time to explain now. Stay exactly where you are and I'll come and fetch you. Don't move. Stay there. Do you understand? I'm on my way. Stay where you are. (*Puts the phone down.*) There's not a moment to lose. I've got to get to Swanker before they do. I'll be taking my cocoa late tonight Mrs H. I'm off on a life and death mission to a secret location in central London.

MRS HORROCKS: Now, did you get the address this time, Mr Barton?

DICK BARTON: Ah.

(*The phone rings again. He snatches it up.*)

SWANKER: I'm at the Colony Rooms.

DICK BARTON: Thank you very much.

BBC ANNOUNCER: And so our story whisks us to the Colony Rooms in darkest Soho. The innocent Swanker chatters with the proprietress as he waits for his famous pal, blissfully unaware that he risks death at the hands of EFIL and food poisoning from the bar snacks.

(*The Colony Rooms. SWANKER sitting at the bar. With a small case at his side. The stickers indicate he's travelled from Cairo. MURIEL BELCHER is serving him. She has a cockney accent.*)

SWANKER: Muriel, you're looking even lovelier than I remembered.

MURIEL: 'Ere I want none of your bleedin' guff young man. You swan in here after ten years without so much as a postcard of the Taj Mahal.

SWANKER: That's in India, Muriel. I was in the desert kingdoms most of the time.

MURIEL: You can buy a postcard of the Taj Mahal anywhere.

SWANKER: Good point.

MURIEL: It's lovely to see you though duck. 'Ere, in honour of the occasion why don't you have a shot of this? I got it on the black market. It'll knock your socks off.

(*She pours him a shot of liquor. He knocks it back and reels from the impact.*)

SWANKER: Great heavens!

MURIEL: Good init? Fancy a porky scratching?

(*She ducks down behind the bar to fetch the bar snack. While she's not looking SWANKER takes the opportunity to steal another shot which he knocks back. Scary underscoring. The MUMMY appears behind the bar in MURIEL's place. SWANKER does a double take from the shot glass to the MUMMY.*)

SWANKER: My God this stuff's good. May I?

(*The MUMMY makes a lurch for him but he moves to pick up the bottle and, unaware, escapes. Knocks back another shot from the bottle.*)

God, you look gorgeous tonight, Muriel. 'Muriel Belcher', what poetry there is in that name.

(*He sings, moving out of range of the MUMMY.*)

A Rhyme for Muriel

'MURIEL BELCHER'
A NAME THAT MAKES ME
WANT TO WRITE A SONNET.
'MURIEL BELCHER'
WHAT POETRY A MAN COULD BASE UPON IT.
IT'S A NAME TO INSPIRE THE ANGELS
ALTHOUGH I CAN FORESEE A LITTLE HITCH.
WHAT RHYMES WITH MURIEL?
UNLESS YOU CALL ON WORDS LIKE
WELL...TUTORIAL.
WHAT RHYMES WITH MURIEL?
AND COULD I COMPARE THEE TO A SUMMER'S ORIEL?
TONSORIAL AND BOREAL
HARDLY ARE SENSORIAL...

(*As the song continues there are moments when SWANKER stands still, lost in thought, and then just as the MUMMY is about to grab him he suddenly moves off inspired by another rhyme and oblivious to the danger he is in.*)

OR TERPSICHORIAL.
THEY'RE NOT MEMORIAL
AND JUST NOT POETICAL
THEY SIMPLY WILL NOT DO AT ALL.
SO ARBOREAL?
AMBASSADORIAL AND CORDIAL.
PERHAPS SARTORIAL.
LEGISLATORIAL IS WRONG.
ADVERBIAL, CONNUBIAL,
ARMORIAL, TUTORIAL,
VISORIAL AND CEREAL
ARE HARDLY FITTING FOR A SONG.

(*Whilst the MUMMY tries unsuccessfully to grab SWANKER, PIGGY and NEFATARTIE sneak on at the back and snatch his suitcase. NEFATARTIE collects the MUMMY and they all exit.*)

ENCHORIAL, MARMOREAL,
GRESSORIAL, CURSORIAL,

SCANSORIAL, AUCTORIAL
FOSSORIAL, RAPTORIAL?
IT'S A PUZZLEMENT INDEED
BUT I'LL GLADLY CARRY ON
SEARCHING FOR THE WORDS I NEED
BUT...OH DEAR I SEE YOU'VE GONE.

(*DICK BARTON and JOCK rush in.*)

DICK BARTON: Swanker!

SWANKER: Babs!

DICK BARTON: Are you alright? We saw Piggy's car speeding away just as we arrived.

SWANKER: Old Piggy Petherington was here?

DICK BARTON: Yes, but I'm afraid he's met a loose woman and gone to the bad. I was worried that he might kill you to get his hands on the map of the Colossus' tomb.

SWANKER: Piggy? Kill me...What a ridiculous...No, I'm fine. I was just having a little drink with Muriel. And the map's safely locked in my case right h...Good gracious. My case. It's gone.

DICK BARTON: Are you sure?

SWANKER: Absolutely, it was on the floor here.

DICK BARTON: Dash it all, we can't let Piggy and his gal get the treasure. That ruby could finance foreign infamy for decades to come.

SWANKER: But I'm afraid they've got the only copy of the map.

DICK BARTON: You must remember some of it.

SWANKER: Oh yes, I studied it for hours but the last time I went for a stroll in the desert without a map I got lost and had to live for ten years as an Arab. It wouldn't have been so bad except for the first three years the sheik appointed me head wife.

DICK BARTON: I'd keep that to yourself if I were you.

JOCK: What are we going to do?

DICK BARTON: There is only one thing to do. We pack a case and head off after the blaggards. (*To SWANKER.*) Could your RAF chums get us back to Cairo?

SWANKER: I know there's some fellows flying out at noon tomorrow.

DICK BARTON: Not till noon. Dash it, that'll give Piggy a hell of a head start. But perhaps they'll take their time. We have the element of surprise in our favour.

(*JOCK blows into a paper bag, inflating it.*)

SWANKER: 'The e – lement of surprise.' How exactly does that work?

(*JOCK bursts the paper bag – bang!*)

I see. Thank you very much.

DICK BARTON: Well, the delay'll give us a chance to swap news over a light supper. Jock, you go and start packing. I'll need four pairs of khaki shorts, a change of evening wear, my mackintosh in case it gets chilly, my beige trilby and a panama hat.

JOCK: Are you taking the pith?

DICK BARTON: Pardon!

(*JOCK holds up a pith helmet.*)

JOCK: Oh I see. Yes, jolly good idea. So Swanker are you ready for the best slap up nosh London has to offer?

SWANKER: Rather!

JOCK: Splendid. Jock, give him your ration card.

(*JOCK sadly hands it over. DICK BARTON leads SWANKER out.*)

DICK BARTON: (*Casually.*) So tell me a bit more about this head wife business.

BBC ANNOUNCER: Packed and ready for the long flight to Egypt, Piggy Petherington and Queen Nefatartie indeed arrive in Africa before Dick Barton and his trusty band of hale fellows well met. Home again on her dirty native soil, the ruthless foreign strumpet wastes no time in hiring the most powerful Nile cruiser and with all motors roaring they head up the mighty river in the direction of the tomb of the Colossus of Cartouche.

(*PIGGY and NEFATARTIE are looking over the rail of their boat.*)

NEFATARTIE: Faster! Faster! Can't we make this tub of crap go any faster?

PIGGY: The engines are running at full capacity, oh sand in my eye.

NEFATARTIE: I told you we should have got one powered by slaves. But no, you had to get a boat from those queer English guys.

PIGGY: I think they were jolly kind to us. It's mid-week at the height of the tourist season, all the other cruisers have set off for Luxor. This was the only one left because it's too small and powerful for tourists.

NEFATARTIE: I've had faster dandruff.

PIGGY: Darling look at the view, it's so beautiful here. Don't you want to be a little romantic? Wouldn't you like to 'make out'?

NEFATARTIE: This is the land of mighty deserts, of timeless mystery, of a great river endlessly flowing to the fathomless depths of sparkling seas. We journey onwards to the final resting place of the greatest lover of all time. Every cry of the eagles above us transports me back to the ecstasies we reached, every sigh of the gentle wind through the bullrushes recalls his hot breath on my neck, every plunge of the bow through the water reminds me of the motion of our lovemaking throughout the long, hot, dark velvet night. (*Breaking the spell.*) And you think I wanna go below deck and tug at *your* little weenie?

PIGGY: That's not a terribly nice thing to say. You couldn't keep your hands off me in London.

NEFATARTIE: Jeez London! Can you blame me for being bored!

PIGGY: I'm beginning to think mother was right. You're nothing more than a gold-digger.

NEFATARTIE: What a limited imagination that old broad has. I'm much greedier than that. And once I get my ruby back I won't have to suck up to any man ever again, including you. So if you wanna stay along for the ride you'd better make yourself useful and get this crock to go faster.

PIGGY: I tell you we're at full capacity.

NEFATARTIE: Well, I'm feeling like I've reached capacity too.

PIGGY: What do you mean?

NEFATARTIE: I've had my fill of you.

PIGGY: It's not my fault. Perhaps if you hadn't lumbered us with so much excess baggage we could go a little faster.

NEFATARTIE: Oh, my thoughts too! (*She calls.*) Tuten!

PIGGY: What are you calling him for?

(*The MUMMY appears.*)

NEFATARTIE: Tuten honey, Piggy-Wiggy here thinks we're carrying a little too much baggage on this trip. Won't you help him lighten our load?

(*We hear an almighty splash as PIGGY is thrown overboard.*)

BBC ANNOUNCER: Poor Piggy, thrown into the unforgiving currents of the Nile, will his life flash before him as the deep waters swallow him? Will he rue the day when he decided to take up with a foreigner? Meanwhile, our heroes set off for Egypt, courtesy of our plucky lads in the RAF. On arrival however they too have difficulty finding a boat and are directed to the offices of the mysterious Englishmen.

(*JOCK, SWANKER and DICK BARTON in an office in Cairo.*)

JOCK: Och, it's hotter than Granny McNair's porridge.

DICK BARTON: Of course it's hot Jock, otherwise there'd be no opportunity to wear khaki shorts, would there? Anyway it's cooler in here with the ceiling fan.

JOCK: I think I might just lie down underneath it. (*He does so.*)

SWANKER: What is this place? (*Reads.*) 'Never fear, tourists dear, we speak only English here.'

(*RODGER and WILCO, the gay secret agents, arrive. They're not camp, rather they're very bluff and hearty.*)

RODGER: Dicky Barton!

WILCO: How are you old chap?

DICK BARTON: (*Delighted to see them.*) My goodness me, it's Rodger and Wilco – Britain's finest secret agents and show-tune aficionados. What brings you to Egypt?

WILCO: We're down here on a ripping secret mission, aren't we darling?

RODGER: We certainly are Wiggy! This office is our cover, do you like it?

WILCO: Rodgina picked out all the colour schemes.

DICK BARTON: What's the mission?

RODGER: All terribly hush-hush. Something about a dam at Aswan, international banana tariffs and sewage.

WILCO: 'SUEZ' darling 'SUEZ'. Do try and get it right.

RODGER: Sorry old girl. (*To the visitors.*) We're awaiting further instructions.

RODGER: Meanwhile we just have to hang around here and blend in.

WILCO: We've started a little business hiring out deckchairs to the English visitors – waterwings, motor launches, that kind of thing.

SWANKER: Motor launches! Could you find one for us? We've got to get down the Nile, it's an absolute tippity-top emergency.

WILCO: Well, we'd love to help old boy but we hired out the last fast boat around here to a flustered podgy chap and a Rita Hayworth type. I don't want to seem ungallant but she was bit of a potty mouth.

SWANKER: That sounds like...

DICK BARTON: We have to catch up with them.

RODGER: No chance I'm afraid. They set off at a fair old lick. They'll be miles away now. You can either take a sailboat or wait for a cruiser at the end of the week.

SWANKER: This is a disaster!

WILCO: I say Rodge. There's a dead Scotsman under the ceiling fan. Is he one of yours?

RODGER: I was about to ask you the same thing.

DICK BARTON: He's with us.

WILCO: Fancy.

DICK BARTON: Just a minute. You haven't got another of those ceiling fans around have you?

WILCO: I'll have a look out the back. (*He exits.*)

SWANKER: What do you want that for, Babs?

DICK BARTON: A propeller.

EVERYONE: What!

DICK BARTON: We'll need a few more items as well if this is going to work.

RODGER: Well, name them and we'll see what we can do.

JOCK: Och, I love it when he gets that wee glint in his eye.

DICK BARTON: There's no time to lose. The first thing we need is a lawnmower and a large industrial-strength elastic band.

BBC ANNOUNCER: (*Atmospherically.*) Night falls across the mysterious land of the pharaohs. In Cairo, Dick Barton beavers away at his contraption with his chums. Even his elegant schoolfriend has no thoughts of swanking tonight. Further down the Nile, that coursing lifeblood of this mighty desert kingdom, the ruthless Queen Nefatartie looks up at the stars and dreams of lost love, little suspecting our boys will soon be in hot pursuit.

(*In the moonlight on the deck of her boat NEFATARTIE sings like Sarah Brightman.*)

Out Of The Past

NEFATARTIE: (*Sings.*)

> OUT OF THE PAST YOU TOUCH ME
> SOMEHOW YOUR ARMS SURROUND ME
> ACROSS THE YEARS YOU'VE FOUND ME
> HOW COULD I FEEL ALONE?
> I KNOW IT'S SELF-DELUSION
> HOW CAN WE EVER TOUCH
> YET AS THE DARK ENFOLDS ME
> I FEEL YOUR LOVE SO MUCH.
> OUR TIME HAS PASSED
> YET STILL I FEEL
> YOUR LOVE CAN TOUCH MY HEART.

(*The music swells. The BBC ANNOUNCER is almost in tears. He sings with her in beautiful harmony.*)

BOTH: (*Sing.*)

OUR TIME HAS PASSED
YET STILL I FEEL
(*Big mushy finish.*)
YOUR LOVE CAN TOUCH MY HEART.

(*Lights down on her. The BBC ANNOUNCER is crying through the applause then pulls himself together.*)

BBC ANNOUNCER: Back in Cairo dawn breaks and our unsleeping heroes survey the fruits of their night's labours. The flying machine is ready. It's over and out to Rodger and Wilco and up, up and away to adventure for Dick Barton and his chums.

(*We see DICK BARTON and SWANKER in the cockpit of the plane with JOCK clinging on to the tail or wing.*)

Barton is Your Man

ALL THREE: (*Sing.*)

OH WE'RE ENGLISHMUN
AND WE'RE OFF ON AN ADVENTURE
YES WE'RE ENGLISHMUN
AND WE GIVE IT ALL WE CAN –

JOCK: (*Sings.*)

WELL, TECHNICALLY I'M SCOTTISH –

DICK BARTON: (*Sings.*)

OH NOW JOCK, DON'T BE PEDANTIC
FOR THE PURPOSE OF THIS PROJECT
YOU CAN JOIN OUR CLAN.

ALL THREE: (*Sing.*)

OH WE'RE ENGLISHMUN
PROPER, PUCKER, BEST OF BRITISH.
STERLING ENGLISHMUN

DICK BARTON: (*Sings.*)

I'M BRITANNIA'S FAV'RITE SON
JOHNNY FOREIGNER WON'T HANG AROUND

AND HELP YOU WHEN THE CHIPS ARE DOWN
YOU'RE BETTER FAR RELYING ON AN ENGLISHMUN.

ALL THREE: (*Sing.*)

WE'RE RIDICULOUSLY DARING
AND WE'RE ENGLISHMUN
WE'RE INSENSITIVE, UNCARING
BUT WE'RE ENGLISHMUN
WE DON'T KNOW WHAT WE'RE DOING
BUT IF TROUBLE'S EVER BREWING
YOU CAN BET THAT IN THE MIDDLE
WE'LL BE ENGLISHMUN.

OH WE'RE ENGLISHMUN
THOUGH THE EMPIRE'S GETTING SMALLER
STILL WE'RE ENGLISHMUN
AND WE'RE NEVER, EVER WRONG
THOUGH WE MAY NOT BE THE BRIGHTEST
STILL OUR MANNERS ARE THE NICEST
AND THAT'S THE MOST IMPORTANT
THING TO ENGLISHMUN.

(*Lights down on them and up on the BBC ANNOUNCER.*)
BBC ANNOUNCER: (*Sings.*)

IF YOU'RE STUCK IN A STICKY SPOT
OR THEY'VE CAUGHT YOU IN A TRAP
THERE'S ONE LAST HOPE YOU'VE GOT
DICK BARTON IS THE CHAP

IF YOU'RE IN A FRIGHTFUL BIND
AND YOUR PIG IS IN A POKE
I GUARANTEE YOU'LL FIND
DICK BARTON IS YOUR BLOKE

(*DICK BARTON, SWANKER and JOCK sing with him.*)
ALL FOUR: (*Sing.*)

HE'S THE HERO OF THE HOUR
WITH SO MANY QUALITIES
HE'S A FORCE FOR THE GOOD
A NEW ROBIN HOOD
A TEA-TIME HERCULES

SO IF YOU'RE EVER IN DESPAIR
AND WITHOUT A RESCUE PLAN
JUST CALL AND HE'LL BE THERE
DICK BARTON IS YOUR
(*Little segue into* What shall we do with the Drunken Sailor.)
EVERY EVENING ON HIS SHOW HE
TRIES TO HELP THE WEAK AND LOWLY

JOCK: (*Sings.*)

WITH THE HELP OF JOCK AND SNOWY
(*And back to* Life on the Ocean Wave *for a big finish.*)
DICK BARTON IS YOUR –
BARTON IS YOUR
BARTON IS YOUR MAN!

BBC ANNOUNCER: Barton and co. soon overtake Queen Nefatartie's boat. They find the burial chamber beneath a mountain at the coordinates etched into Swanker's memory by his long hours tossing through sweaty sleepless nights. And so it is Dick Barton and his crew who are the first living creatures to disturb the silence of the tomb and probe the fathomless mysteries of the ancient dead.
(*The interior of the Colossus' tomb. DICK BARTON, SWANKER and JOCK step into the scene.*)

JOCK: So if they didn't have fridges how do they keep the milk cold?

SWANKER: This is extraordinary. If I hadn't won the map in a spirited game of Bedouin backgammon, it could have lain undiscovered for all time.

DICK BARTON: We must remember that this is the final resting place of a fellow human being. This chap once lived and breathed, loved, lost and laughed as we do. We must afford his grave the highest respect.

JOCK: What do you mean?

DICK BARTON: We must get the fellow on display at the British Museum in time for the school holidays.

SWANKER: (*Reverently.*) I'm sure it's what he would have wanted.

DICK BARTON: Now, where's the ruby?

SWANKER: Fellows of this class often had their most precious possession buried in the sarcophagus with them.

DICK BARTON: Let's open it up and have a look.

(*They move towards the sarcophagus.*)

On second thoughts, it could very well be booby-trapped. We must exercise extreme caution. Jock, open it would you?

JOCK: Right you are DB. (*He prises open the lid.*)

(*JOCK is appalled at what he sees.*)

Och no! Poor laddie!

DICK BARTON: What is it Jock?

JOCK: No wonder he died. They've cut off his…his…His 'you know what' is missing.

DICK BARTON: What are you talking about, man?

JOCK: His 'you know'. His 'wee timorous beastie'.

DICK BARTON: What?

JOCK: His 'Monarch Of The Glen', his 'Sporran Spanner' His 'Haggis Handle' –

DICK BARTON: Yes, we get the general picture now, thank you. Let me have a look.

(*BARTON and SWANKER look.*)

Great heavens!

SWANKER: Just a moment, there's a hieroglyph here. I know this script. It says: 'He who was a Colossus in life, in death is humbled.'

DICK BARTON: He certainly is. Let's give the fellow a little dignity. (*He removes his pith helmet and apparently places it over the MUMMY's missing bits.*)

SWANKER: 'Close by lies his bountiful blessings in offering to the gods.'

DICK BARTON: Good heavens. Does that mean there's a separate coffin for the fellow's manhood?

SWANKER: Not exactly a coffin, in some obscure cults it was customary to make an offering to the gods of one's greatest blessings. These were then placed in a special casket to insure they remained undamaged in the journey to the underworld.

DICK BARTON: Rather unusual for a chap to regard his most precious possession as his –

JOCK: I disagree boss. There was fellow from Dundee in our battalion who could balance a teapot on the end of his and he said –

DICK BARTON: This is no time to relate your National Service high jinks, man!

SWANKER: I'll wager the ruby is buried with this fellow's –

DICK BARTON: Colossus.

SWANKER: Exactly. I daresay there's some fiendish puzzle lost in the complexities of these ancient wall carvings which may provide some slight clue to the intricate hiding place of the casket. At last a chance to put to use my years of study of ancient texts and burial customs.

(JOCK emerges carrying a very obviously phallic-shaped casket.)

JOCK: Is this it?

SWANKER: Might be.

(They open the box. Again we can't see inside it. Red light glows up into their faces.)

Well, there's the ruby. It's actually been imbedded into the end of the –

DICK BARTON: What an extraordinary mounting. It's a magnificent specimen.

JOCK: It's the biggest one I've ever seen.

DICK BARTON: There'll be queues around the block when this fellow goes on display in Bloomsbury.

SWANKER: We don't have much time, Queen Nafatartie and her creatures could arrive at any moment. I wager she'll fight to the death to get her hands on this again.

DICK BARTON: Good thinking. Jock you stand guard outside, I'll radio through to the British embassy and tell them what we've found.

SWANKER: I'll see if I can decipher any more ancient secrets locked in the hieroglyphics around these walls.

JOCK: There's a lovely recipe for cheese scones over there by the door.

(SWANKER deliberately looks at the opposite wall.)

That's just a lot of boring stuff about splitting the atom.

DICK BARTON: To your post please Jock, I'm sure we can leave the Egyptology to the experts.

JOCK: (*Cheerfully leaving.*) Righty-ho DB!

DICK BARTON: Keep your wits about you old boy.

(*He leaves. When SWANKER is turned away the MUMMY of the Colossus sits up in the sarcophagus and clambers out with DICK BARTON's pith helmet still preserving his modesty. He lumbers toward SWANKER. SWANKER turns and screams. The MUMMY grabs him round the throat and is throttling him. Then SNOWY appears through the trap door with his face still bandaged up.*)

SNOWY: Alright me old cock. Sorry to interrupt but I'm looking for me boss Dick Barton and me old mucker, Jock. I've got a very urgent note for the guv. (*Puts the letter down.*) Blimey those catacombs are dusty, I never thought I'd find you. I'm Snowy. How you diddling? (*SWANKER is wheezing and coughing.*)

SWANKER: Get help, quickly.

(*The main theme from Tchaikovsky's* Romeo and Juliet *plays as the MUMMY turns to look at SNOWY's bandaged face.*)

SNOWY: 'Ere have you got this skin complaint as well? Don't these bandages itch? Looks like yours could with a change me old mate!

(*The MUMMY growls lustfully at SNOWY.*)

What's the matter with him? Don't he like me?

SWANKER: On the contrary. I think he likes you rather too much. I should run for it if I were you!

(*The MUMMY has his back to the audience. He looks down at the pith helmet hanging between his legs. He roars and throws it aside. He picks up the phallic casket and advances on SNOWY. SNOWY, terrified, backs towards the wall.*)

SNOWY: 'Ere no mate. I think you've got the wrong idea. I'm not that way inclined! (*He backs into the wall and a secret panel slides open. There are steps inside.*) Where does this lead?

SWANKER: Up onto the mountain I think.

SNOWY: Get the guv and Jock to rescue me.

(*The MUMMY chases SNOWY out and up. NEFATARTIE appears.*)

NEFATARTIE: Who are you? How did you reach this place before me?

SWANKER: We meet again Marta Heartburn. Can it be ten years since you stole that sapphire from me in a Budley Salterton bordello?

NEFATARTIE: Cut the dramatics whoever you are and hand over the ruby.

SWANKER: It's not here.

NEFATARTIE: What do you mean, it's not here. That ruby's mine I tell you. I gave it to my darling Colossus and he promised he'd hide it for eternity where no man would touch it.

SWANKER: Few men, but many women.

NEFATARTIE: (*She pulls out a gun.*) Enough of these riddles. Prepare to die!

SWANKER: Don't shoot! The treasure and the mutated creature that you seek are up on the mountain top.

NEFATARTIE: My honey-bun lives! How is his mutation after all these centuries?

SWANKER: Still pretty spectacular.

NEFATARTIE: Get out of my way.

(*She exits through the panel up to the mountain. DICK BARTON and JOCK enter through the main door.*)

DICK BARTON: Swanker, are you alright? What's all the commotion?

SWANKER: Your cock-er-ney assistant's here. He's brought you an urgent note from London.

DICK BARTON: (*Snatches up the note and rips it open to read.*) Thank heavens he did. It's from Mrs Perkins the newsagent. I left home without cancelling the papers. Where's Snowy now?

SWANKER: Out on the mountain being pursued by an amorous corpse.

DICK BARTON: I've never known Snowy attract an admirer.

SWANKER: I think after centuries of going without it the mummy was just happy to see another mummy.

DICK BARTON: Extraordinary business. Just a minute, what's that smell of heavy perfume?

SWANKER: That's the other thing. Nefatartie has arrived, she's gone out after the ruby.

DICK BARTON: We can't let international crime monopolise that magnificent object.

(*SNOWY arrives.*)

JOCK: Snowy, are you alright?

SNOWY: Right lads! Phew that was a narrow escape and no mistake, I thought I was done for.

DICK BARTON: Forgetting to cancel the papers is hardly life and death.

SNOWY: Nah, not that – being pursued by that big bugger in the bandages.

SWANKER: What's going on up there now?

SNOWY: They're having a little chat, like. Something about summoning the armies of the living dead to roll a boulder in front of the door, flooding the catacombs and sending a fireball down the secret passage.

DICK BARTON: Great heavens, we're in mortal danger.

JOCK: Not if we follow the instructions on the wall. There's a system for repelling invaders. The lever behind the sarcophagus causes a series of tunnels in the mountain to collapse, undermining the surface layer and sending whoever's above us to a certain death in the chasm below.

SWANKER: How does he know all theses things?

DICK BARTON: Evening classes in advanced hieroglyphics. He couldn't get on the woodwork course, though. Ask him to put up some shelves and it's a whole different matter.

SNOWY: Well done, Jock.

DICK BARTON: There's only one problem with this scheme.

SWANKER: What's that?

DICK BARTON: I didn't think of it.

SWANKER: No one need ever know.

DICK BARTON: Jock?

JOCK: Yes DB.

DICK BARTON: Sign me up for flower arranging and eighteenth-century cake decorating as soon as we get home. You can never tell when that kind of information could save the day.

JOCK: Right you are.

DICK BARTON: We'd better find this lever then.

SNOWY: Here it is.

JOCK: Who's going to do the honours?

SWANKER: I've always had an unusually strong wrist action.

DICK BARTON: From the look of things, it's going to need an almighty yank from all of us.

(They all attempt to pull the lever.)

JOCK: It's not budging DB!

DICK BARTON: Come along everyone. I want you to all pull together for England –

(They tug – nothing.)

The Empire –

(Again – nothing.)

Little Princess Margaret Rose.

(A huge effort from the boys shifts the lever. Blackout. A huge roar of the mountain collapsing above. Lights up on the same scene as before. We hear DICK BARTON approaching from offstage.)

(Off.) Snowy, see if you can get the engine started for home.

SNOWY: *(Off.)* Righty-ho, boss.

(DICK BARTON, JOCK and SWANKER enter looking stunned.)

SWANKER: What a terrible way to die.

JOCK: The poor wee lassie.

SWANKER: Impaled on a jewel-encrusted mummified phallus.

DICK BARTON: Do you know, in so many ways I think it's how she would have wanted to go. Did any of you notice the expression on her face?

SWANKER/JOCK: No.

DICK BARTON: I suppose that's what marks me out as a trained secret agent. She looked remarkably serene, as if she'd finally come home. Pray God her tortured soul rests in peace now.

SWANKER: Well Barbara, I suppose it's back to dear old Blighty for us now. I think my travelling days are over. Time to settle down in the old country and give something back to the Motherland.

DICK BARTON: What will you do, old chum?

SWANKER: I'm not sure yet, perhaps run for Parliament, begin blowing a definitive collection of wild birds' eggs, or found a hostel for fallen women and distressed seamen in the East End.

DICK BARTON: It's good to have a calling. I think we've learnt a great deal on this adventure, eh Jock?

JOCK: What would that be DB?

DICK BARTON: (*Churchillian.*) The lessons we learnt on the playing fields of public school are as true today as they were then. Fair play and a straight bat are all you ever need for a sticky wicket.

JOCK: And to bowl a maiden over.

DICK BARTON: I think we've extended the cricketing metaphor quite far enough now thank you, Jock.
(*PIGGY arrives brandishing a gun.*)

PIGGY: Aren't you forgetting something Barton!

SWANKER: Piggy!

DICK BARTON: What would that be, Petherington?

PIGGY: All the fat boys who never got picked for the first eleven. It's time we wiped the smile off all your smug faces.

DICK BARTON: Remember the immortal credo by which we lived our nubile young lives – 'matron doesn't like a bad loser'.

PIGGY: Matron can't help you now Barton, no one can. I've been humiliated by the woman I loved, tossed into the swirling waters of the mighty Nile by a stinking corpse, wrestled for my life with crocodiles, survived in a desert wilderness on nuts, berries and Kendle mint cake, befriended a nomadic leper colony and trained them into a crack fighting unit. The lepers surround every known entrance to this tomb, a dozen men deep. There is no other possible way out, in, under or around us. You are completely at my mercy. Experience the fear of the podgy first-year boarder about to have his head flushed down the cricket pavilion lavatory. Prepare to die.

SWANKER: (*To DICK BARTON.*) Good God old man. What are you going to do?

JOCK: How are you going to get out of this one, Barbara?

DICK BARTON: There's only one way to find out.

SWANKER/JOCK: How?

BBC ANNOUNCER: Tune in to the next exciting episode of –

EVERYONE: Dick Barton – Special Agent

The End.